COMMISSIONING OF
OFFSHORE OIL
AND GAS PROJECTS

COMMISSIONING OF OFFSHORE OIL AND GAS PROJECTS

THE MANAGER'S HANDBOOK

2nd edition

A strategic and tactical guide to the successful planning and execution of the commissioning of large complex offshore facilities

Trond Bendiksen & Geoff Young

authorHOUSE®

AuthorHouse™
1663 Liberty Drive
Bloomington, IN 47403
www.authorhouse.com
Phone: 1-800-839-8640

Published by AuthorHouse 03/24/2015

ISBN: 978-1-4969-6053-5 (sc)
ISBN: 978-1-4969-6052-8 (e)

Library of Congress Control Number: 2015900175

Print information available on the last page.

Any people depicted in stock imagery provided by Thinkstock are models,
and such images are being used for illustrative purposes only.
Certain stock imagery © Thinkstock.

This book is printed on acid-free paper.

Notes to 2nd .edition:

This is the 2nd edition of the book. It has been completely revised and updated from the 1st edition with
new advice based on current best practices, new and revised illustrations, additional industry data,
new process tools etc., which makes the book more comprehensive and more user-friendly.

Trond Bendiksen

Trond Bendiksen has 35 years of experience in the Oil and Gas industry in the North Sea, Eastern Canada and the US. He has worked with all the major oil companies on GBS's, Jackets, Floating Production Units (PFU's, FPSO's) and has completion experience from a vast amount of mega-projects. He has solid project and operational experience from a variety of management positions including Offshore Operations Manager on several platforms.

His involvement in Business Process Re-engineering projects and high level world wide Benchmarking studies has given him a unique insight into the organizational aspects of the job that is so important for the success of a project.

He has also published books on Continuous Improvement Techniques, Business Process Mapping and Analysis as well as several papers on Organizational Effectiveness.

He conducts international courses on the subjects of Project Management, Commissioning Management and Business Process Improvement.

TB is a Norwegian citizen currently residing in Norway as a senior business advisor to a variety of offshore operators nationally and internationally.

Geoff Young

Geoff Young has 40 years of experience in the Oil and Gas industry in the North Sea and worldwide.He has worked with all major oil companies on GBS's, Jackets, Floating Production units(FPU's), FPSO's and onshore facilities, and has completion experience from a vast amount of mega-projects, both as a senior commissioning engineer and senior planner.

GY has gained significant experience in commissioning planning and estimating through his long career in the UK, Holland, Belgium, Saudi Arabia, Norway, the US and Canada.

GY is one of the few Senior Planners that can actually do all the initial planning, drawing mark-ups, estimating etc. on his own as the first cut of the schedule/budget before the commissioning engineers are recruited. An extremely rare and valuable skill not easily found in the industry.

GY is a UK citizen currently residing in Western Canada as a senior advisor to a variety of operators.

Acknowledgements

In compiling this work we have sought advice and guidance from a number of individuals and sources but principally the greatest assistance has been provided by our own working colleagues on a variety of projects.

We would especially like to acknowledge the guidance provided by Ed Martin and Gordon Carrick of Petro-Canada (now Nalcor and Suncor) who took the time to thoroughly read the whole manuscript of the first edition, and offered valuable comments on the content, structure and layout.

We have had many discussions with quite a few of our colleagues on the subjects discussed in this book, which have directly affected the quality of the content. They are too many to mention, so this is to all of you; thank you very much!

Once a robust draft of this second edition of the book was completed, several people contributed their time in reviewing, commenting and making suggestions for improvements. This has specifically contributed to the betterment of the final product.

We will specifically thank Oddvar Berge and Rolf Jacobsen for their professional contributions.

A great many thanks also to Benedicte Holgersen, Eirik Soensteboe and Odin Folke Olsen who so professionally and expediently upgraded all illustrations from the first edition, and to Malin Eide who helped out with editing the first draft of this second edition.

Preface

This book is specifically directed at Commissioning Managers, Project Managers and Senior Project Planners. It will also provide valuable and useful information that will assist Engineering Managers, Construction Managers, Commissioning Leads and Commissioning Engineers in performing their jobs.

The concept of the book has been to break the commissioning activity down into four main phases, namely; 1) Planning, 2) Preparations, 3) Execution and 4) Documentation, Hand-Over and Take Over.

The goal has been to identify the main areas where managers need to keep their focus- the key success factors - in order to prevent schedule and budget overruns. We have chosen to narrow the focus down to the single most important elements of each of the four main phases; those that contribute the most, and hence can make or break a project.

Contrary to what one might think, it is not the delay of major project milestones such as sail-away from module yards, module lift at integration site or delays in offshore laying activities that constitute the major delay factors on a project. It is all the other important big or small issues that pop up along the way and materialize during commissioning, that you have not properly prepared for that make the biggest difference.

This book also provides some very accurate experience data on what you can expect in terms of potentially overrunning your initial estimates if you don't seriously pick up on, and resolve the issues dealt with herein. Figures quoted in this book reflect multi-module large projects.

Smaller projects have the same issues, but figures may have to be scaled down to suit. The book focuses only on the key issues that you need to resolve and does not provide specific references or recommendations as to specific tools and equipment.

We have tried to put the issues in a Continuous Improvement perspective throughout the book in order to encourage you to structure your work in such a way that you always analyze the issues first, then improve and follow up on actions; the Continuous Improvement Circle.

To our knowledge, a book such as this has never been published before. We sincerely think that this book will assist you tremendously in performing your job, and we hope you enjoy reading it as much as we have enjoyed writing it.

Good Luck!
The Authors

PS: *In line with the philosophy described in this book, we are always looking for improvements. If you have any suggestions, comments or questions, please feel free to submit an e-mail to*

trond@bendiksen.net.

Contents

Note on terminology

We have throughout the book used standard industry terminology. We have however experienced confusion on the definition of the term *Handover*. Handover is used differently in various parts of the world. Some places Handover is used to describe two separate events, namely the Handover from Construction to Commissioning as well as Handover from Commissioning to Operations. To avoid confusion we have in this book defined and used Handover as the *Construction to Commissioning transfer*, and the transfer from *Commissioning to Operations we have termed **Take Over**.

Introduction

The Oil & Gas industry continues to display some spectacular overruns on its megaprojects. Just reviewing the overruns on *commissioning hours alone* for a random selection of projects since 1996 and to this day, does not give much hope for the future. It has been a steady overrun increase industrywide year by year and there is no sign of it stopping in the near future. The reasons have not been structurally dealt with, at least not from a strategic and tactical overall project management perspective, and not much literature, if any, exists on the subject of commissioning. We find this quite surprising, considering the importance of the subject and its impact on project completion. Hence this has been our main motivation for writing this book.

To illustrate the fact above, below is the *commissioning* trend in terms of overrun hours as it relates to FPSOs from 1996 to 2014. Based on our investigations, there is not much of a trend difference when it comes to other types of installations such as GB, Steel Jackets, FPU's etc.

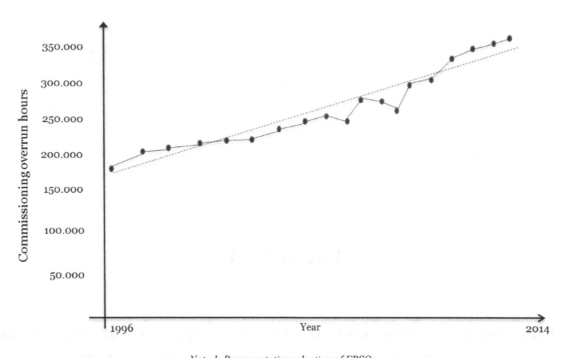

Note 1. Representative selection of FPSOs
Note 2. Checked against fixed installations
Source: Bendiksen & Young BM questionnaire 96-0014

Illustration 1. FPSO commissioning overrun hours trend curve.

Just about any senior manager who has ever been responsible for the Commissioning of a large multi-module mega project knows that, if he/she was not given enough time for planning and preparations, or if the competency of the team was not adequate in the early planning and preparation phase, the likelihood of success is quite slim.

Traditionally commissioning has been viewed as an activity that is executed just before Operations takes over the systems for startup. Quite surprisingly this is still a widely held opinion among Project Managers, not only in Contractors organizations but also inside operating organizations.

Cost (or loss) - analysis very consistently show that it is during commissioning that the loss potential = overrun potential, will manifest itself. This is the phase where design flaws and construction errors will surface, and this is the phase where the expensive and time-consuming changes and modifications will have to be undertaken. Changes and modifications will be executed simultaneously with a very hectic commissioning program, while everyone expects you as the Commissioning Manager to manage and control all this and still deliver on time.

This fact should be the "red flag" for any management team in terms of making sure that commissioning is given the necessary focus from day one of the project.

Commissioning of large multi-module offshore projects is an enormous undertaking that requires significant management skills in a variety of areas, of which communication is a major one. First you need to communicate to the top, the importance of giving commissioning an early start and the benefit of this. Secondly you need to create the vision, goals and strategies for commissioning and then communicate these to your team.

The bottom line results are significant for managers who can successfully create a shared vision of what needs to be done, i.e. believe in the **Plan** that everyone has contributed to developing, confront the team with current realities, and empower the engineers / workers to "go for it". When team members throughout the organization are united by a shared vision and clear goals, it becomes possible to push responsibilities and authorities down the organizational hierarchy to the appropriate level where work is performed. This is the level, which ultimately will have the biggest impact on the bottom line.

This book will help you understand the tremendous value of upfront planning, the importance of risk control during completions, and how organizing the completion team in the right manner will ensure that your project meets the objectives; on schedule and on budget.

We have received a lot of questions as to the overrun hours presented in this book. Most questions have been concerned with why we don't present the *total overruns on projects*, which of course represent much larger numbers than what we show for Commissioning alone. We do of course recognize the question, but the simple answer is that this is a book about Commissioning, and the issues Commissioning can influence, and hence only Commissioning hours are shown and discusses herein.

Ethics and Values

Integrity, ethics and values should be in the forehead of all managers. When the project is at its most hectic, and delays are becoming evident, it can sometimes be difficult to stay calm and maintain integrity and ethical posture.

Here are a few guiding principles for you to remember:

1) The team looks to you for guidance and leadership, give it to them based on honesty and care
2) Always perform honest and accurate reporting, both up and down in the organization.
3) Flag issues early, never hide problems.
4) Be constructive and courteous when criticizing.
5) Praise your team members when works well done.
6) Make sure you base all your actions on facts.
7) Maintain a positive and constructive relationship with all parties you deal with.
8) Don't draw conclusions before you have listened and digested all information provided.
9) Encourage team play, also across organizational boundaries.
10) Ask for, and provide honest feedback on behaviors.

The key to success

The concept of this book has been to break down the commissioning activity down into four main phases, namely; 1) **Planning, 2) Preparations, 3) Execution and 4) Documentation, handover and takeover.**

We have chosen to separate the planning and the preparations activities in two distinctly different phases as the various elements of these are important enough to warrant separate focus and detail discussions.

Before you start reading the various chapters, take a good hard look at the *profile* of the content list of the book below.

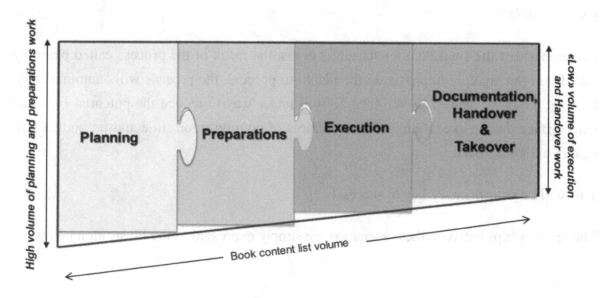

Illustration 2. Book content list profile

The profile simply implies that if you put a lot of thorough quality work into the Planning & Preparations stages, the actual Execution & Doc/Hand-over stages will stand a much better chance of success than if the Planning and Preparations were poor.

Hence the content of this book reflects the same principles.

You will very soon see that the profile you are looking at translates to *the number one key to successful commissioning*, namely **time and resources to conduct enough quality upfront planning and preparations.** In line with this key success factor, the book content list is "front-end loaded"

Our definition of *planning and preparations* is:

All the work, that goes into planning all the required activities to ensure a smooth execution phase with focus on timely handover to Operations.

You will find in this book, unlike a lot of practices out there, that we advocate putting every little thing you'll have to remember to do during execution into the plan, whether it be important stuff such as regular risk session, major Operations Take Over milestones, regulatory witness points or minor stuff such as, flushing witness activities, commissioning and decommissioning of temporaries etc. These we know are not normally found in commissioning schedules, and we also know that for the very same reason, this is a major contributor to schedule delay.

There should be no excuse not to include every activity that requires work and manpower in your schedule!

Remember that the final Plan (or schedule) is just the result of the process called planning, and if you put enough emphasis on the planning process, the process will "automatically" turn out a quality plan! You will then be well under way to reduce the potential risks that may surface during execution and your chances of coming in on time and on budget have significantly improved.

This will be your primary key to success!

The relationships between these scenarios are simply expressed in the illustration below

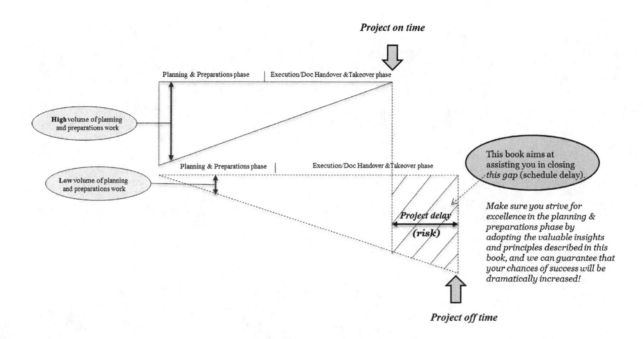

Illustration 3. Planning volume vs risk scenario

1.0 PLANNING

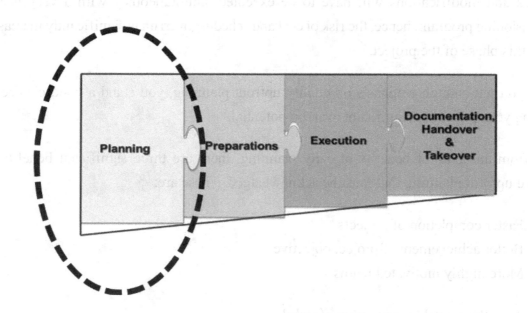

- Planning
- Database systems
- System structure
- The Key Performance Indicators
- Defining the work scope and building the schedule
- Building the schedule
- Commissioning schedule development
- Planning and planning considerations
- Estimating; Strategy, tools and considerations
- Estimating and growth: figures and factors
- Summary: Key Success Factors in the Planning phase

Planning

Planning is a high risk area with a significant financial impact!

Cost, or loss analyses, very consistently show that it is during completion & commissioning that the loss potential = overrun potential will manifest itself.

It is during the Commissioning phase, when the systems come together, that design flaws and construction errors will surface. At this stage, the project will have to undertake expensive and time consuming modifications to correct the problems.

Changes and modifications will have to be executed simultaneously with a very hectic commissioning program; hence, the risk of cost and schedule overrun is significantly increased during this phase of the project.

Unless you put enough emphasis on quality upfront planning, you stand a good chance of exposing your project to significant overrun potential.

Aside from an array of benefits of early planning, there are three significant benefits of effective upfront planning that must be acknowledged. These are;

- Faster completion of projects
- Better achievement of project objective
- More highly motivated teams

Of which all three lead to; *reduction of risks!*

Ultimately however, project planning must be judged on its direct contribution to profits.

Effective front end project planning is a high leverage with a positive financial impact throughout the project life.

In the light of time, cost and other resource constraints, planning is even more essential in order to ensure the most effective use of the resources.

Both the project road map generated by planning and the team building which occurs in developing a successful plan, are necessary precursors for project success.

Who does what, when and with whom?; The "4 W's.

Planning the work is critical to the completion of the project!

Our definition of Planning is; *prerequisites that must be in place in order to develop a quality Plan (schedule)*

In this chapter we will be looking at what you as the manager needs the Project Completion System to do for you, what reports you will need and why you need them, how you want to control the system, and how you want to build the schedule.

We will be discussing essential prerequisites, such as system boundary definitions, commissioning strategy, estimating concepts, numbering concept, temporaries, etc. leading up to a PLAN that can actually be used as a monitoring and control tool as opposed to being a place where you gather historical data.

This chapter will also provide you with some very interesting figures and factors on estimating, growth and expected final completion hours that will assist you in assessing your own project relative to realism and "do ability".

These data has to our knowledge never been officially published before.

We will encourage every manager to apply the KISS (Keep It Simple Stupid) - principle in all aspects of planning as well as for all the other elements of the job!

This does not imply over-simplification, rather a "simple- enough- to –meet the needs" approach.

Database Systems

The databases are pre-requisites to all your planning, scheduling and reporting, so let's start discussing these first.

Regardless of what planning tool, job card system or Project Completion System (PCS) your project has chosen, chances are that they are all interconnected via a huge relationship database structure that's been developed by a computer nerd without the slightest idea of what the actual users – you – require.

Chances are furthermore that the guys on the 50th floor that employ you have decided that this magic tool is mandatory on all their projects. So, if you were thinking of bringing something more simple and user-friendly to the table, forget it!

A relationship database is designed to be flexible and hence can be altered to suit your needs at your request. You can request endless variations of reports and data and you can easily spend the whole day playing around to query whatever you like to see, when and in what fashion.

This is where you will be wasting a lot of time; unless you have PRE-DEFINED what you want to measure and what the basic reports to monitor and control your project should look like. These basic reports are discussed later in this chapter.

Although relationship databases are flexible by nature, it is when you connect these up in a humongous network of different custom built and commercial databases, you might run into problems.

This is discussed next.

System Structure

Chances are that your integrated database structure looks something like the illustration below. Typically the system is made up of a combination of standard tools, like Access, Excel, Primavera, J.D. Edwards, a commercial or custom-built Project Completion System (PCS), a commercial or custom-built Material system, etc. All these elements are then integrated into one huge system.

All of which is supposed to flawlessly come together to give you a tool that you can really depend on.

However, like with all large databases, interface problems are not uncommon. At least you should device a simple back up.

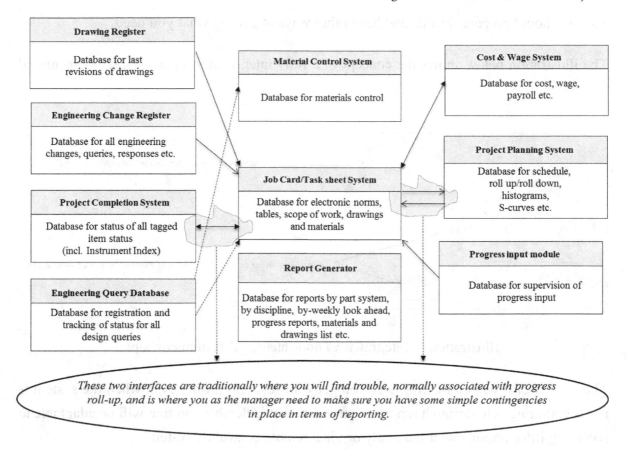

Illustration 4. Database structure overview

We are not advocating that these database systems should not be used. To be perfectly clear; they are tremendously useful! However, we have seen small and big systems failures that have become critical too many times to ignore them. This has especially been the case in remote locations with vulnerable network access where the system relies on a remote server.

In line with the concept of this book we prefer to plan for such events - it is called *risk control*, and hence we device reports that are system independent and can in a worst case be run manually.

You want to make sure you control the system, not the other way around! Again, these systems can be extremely useful as long as they work problem-free. However, experience tells us that we spend, or waste, large amounts of time and resources in trying to fix the system (most specifically interface issues).

Time and resources you don't necessarily control as this is the IT guys' job, but it affects you in as much as you don't get the reports you need to control the job when you need them.

So, you should prepare for this and have other ways of getting what you need.

The illustration below shows the concept of a fully integrated system vs. a semi-integrated system.

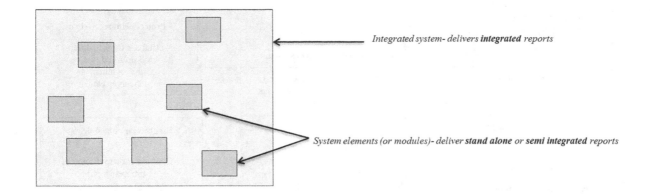

*Integrated system- delivers **integrated** reports*

*System elements (or modules)- deliver **stand alone** or **semi integrated** reports*

Illustration 5. Integrated vs non-integrated system concept

The most useful way of making sure you get your reports on time even when the system is not functioning is to design a reporting structure that is flexible and that will be adaptable to receiving information either manually or via a remote controlled system.

Design your reports for your needs, and not for the system's needs!

The Key Performance Indicators & Report Structure

Before you start the work of building the schedule, it is useful to take some time discussing what performance indicators you will be measured on once the job gets going, and *define your KPI's and Reports up front and make them simple* (KISS).

You as the Manager will be measured against a set of Key Performance Indicators (KPI).

From an Owners viewpoint, the overall KPI is the progressive amount of handed over systems to Operations relative to the planned dates for these, herein referred to as Take Overs. Some refer to as this the *Ultimate KPI* as it reflects the real progress against the Owners expectation.

In order for you to control the work that you are responsible for, you need to establish a set of KPI's for your organization; KPI's that you will monitor regularly as the work progresses.

So first off all you need to define the most important KPI's, those that give you the best indications as to where you stand at all times. Then you need to define the reports that reflect these KPI's. You would want KPI's and reports that not only reflect the Commissioning Team's performance as a whole, but also how the individual Commissioning Leads are performing. There will be several levels of KPI's and hence several levels of reports required to monitor these.

Apart from the endless variety of reports that you will be able to print from the database systems by a touch of a button, there are some very specific reports you will need, that will at a "quick glance" give you the overall status on how you are performing against the agreed KPI's.

Before you start digging away through the mountain of reports your systems will spit out, you need to know the overall picture ("the helicopter view").

The following is a standard, but useful set of KPI's and associated reports you will need:

KPI 1. Amount of Handed Over systems / part systems from Construction to commissioning and in progress by Commissioning. (Hand Overs)

KPI 2. Amount of delayed or advanced Handed Over systems from Construction to Commissioning.

KPI 3. Amount of systems / part systems completed by Commissioning (and Punch List items outstanding).

KPI 4. Amount of systems / part systems fully completed by Commissioning and ready for Hand Over to Operations.

KPI 5. Amount of systems / part systems actually Taken Over by Operations. (Take Overs)

There are obviously a heap of subsets of the above that you will need such as *Punch list status, Design Query status, outstanding Regulatory issues, Preservation status* etc.

Sometimes Operations insists on a minimum number of punch list items and a minimum number of unresolved Design Queries before accepting Take Overs from Commissioning.

In that case you will also have to include KPI's and reports to monitor and reflect these requirement. And not only for reasons regarding Operations acceptance, but also for reasons affecting your acceptance criteria from Construction!

But again;

Make sure you understand the overall picture before you start digging for the details.

When using the reports in your regular status / progress meetings, make sure you graphically visualize all elements of the reports so that the Leads and engineers are fully aware of the status and how their contribution (or lack of) affects the overall picture.

Demand that the Leads explain in writing in their reports, not only the reasons for variations to the plan, but also how they intend to recover from a negative variation!

That puts accountability where it belongs!

Report Levels

The overall (high level) reports can be broken down and produced with various levels of detail depending on whom they are produced for.

The illustration below shows the 3 top levels of "special reports" that you will need to have in place in addition to the standard overall S-curve. We recommend that you specify these, or similar, reports up front. Don't rely on the system giving you these "quick glance" reports once you are well under way. Decide what you want and let your planner devise these simple overall reports.

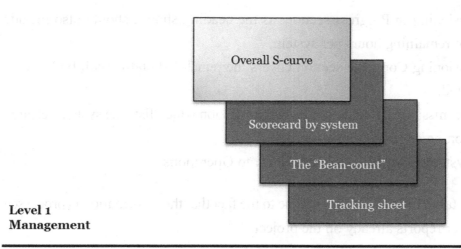

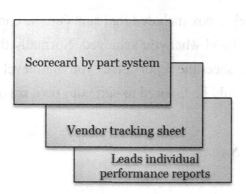

**Level 1
Management**

**Level 2
Leads**

Illustration 6. Report levels

Special Reports- "For Your Eyes Only"

In later sections of this book we will discuss the suite of weekly reports the Project produces to inform all in sundry of the completion status. What you need as the manager is the two-page report that informs you of the status of each system, how your lead engineers are performing and what the status of each of the systems or part systems are.

For this purpose we have designed the following:

The Project Score Card, the Project Tracking Sheet and the Project "Bean Count"

The Project Score Card: This report typically has five sections:

1. Mechanical Completion run from the Construction side of things

2. The Commissioning in Progress section, as the heading shows, should also include the number of remaining hours per system.
3. The Commissioning Complete section covers the punch list status with both "A" & "B" items listed.
4. The fully Commissioned, Ready for Operations section which lists the systems cleared by commissioning.
5. Number of systems/part systems handed over to Operations

This report normally takes little time to set up due to the fact that the information is processed from some of the other reports already on the project.

This report will have a weekly box included that sums up the changes during that week with respect to what you planned and what you achieved. Normally the changes would be shown in 'bold' type and with one sheet the report gives you high level information at a glance. Of course this type of report could be tailored to suit your own set of requirements.

The Project Tracking Sheet

This report is by responsible lead engineer showing part system counts, all associated man-hours with productivity; percentage complete and non-productive time. The questions that you can glean from this report will enable you to pin point any of the troubled systems and how your individual leads are performing. This is a good report to clear out any hold back of progress reporting.

The Project "Bean Count"

This is an overall summary with counts and graphs of all outstanding work from Construction, Commissioning and through to Take Over by Operations. It shows all outstanding Mechanical Completion Certificates, Punch List items, Job cards, Design Queries, Regulatory Punch List items, Commissioning Test Records etc. This overall report shows the trend from week to week and is an excellent tool to keep track of the total status.

We have enhanced the first two reports (Scorecard and Tracking sheet) for each of your lead engineers to allow lower level reporting, producing Score Card by part system, Vendor Tracking sheet and a Leads Individual Performance report.

The Score Card by Part System

This report details the part systems by lead engineer covering scope hours, percent complete, check sheets, and punch list, by-party checks and dossier completions. The report shows what is planned and what is achieved at this level.

The Vendor Tracking Sheet

This report follows the format of the Project tracking sheet showing the major vendor input against the systems.

Leads Individual Performance Reports

This report is produced on a weekly basis following the progress run and it shows the lead engineer's performance for that week. It allows him to monitor his variances and gives a brief explanation for his recovery process. These sections will form a part of the weekly progress report, and being produced directly from the data stored in the computer system it gives your Leads more time in the field. The report also shows the hand over from construction and where potential problems are occurring.

Below is a typical Project Score Card

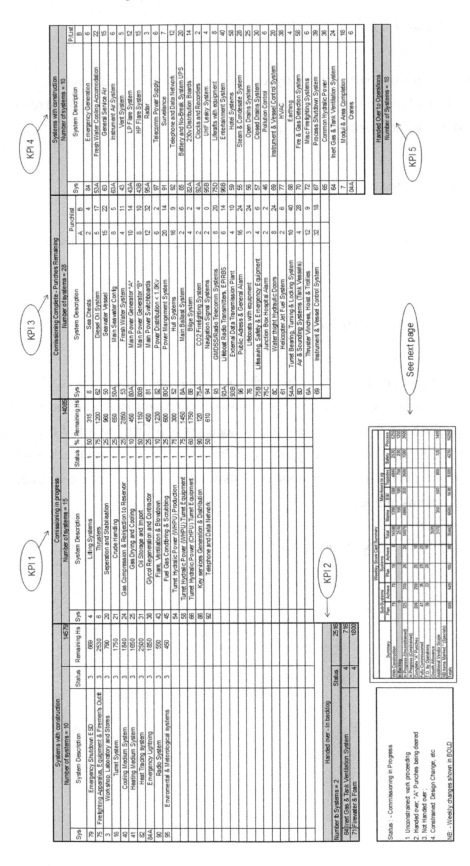

Illustration 7. Typical Project score Card

Below is a typical Weekly Score card Summary

Weekly Score Card Summary

Weekley Score Card Summary

Summary	Sub-Systems		Systems		Total	Man-hours to og				
	Plan	Achieve	Plan	Achieve		Marine	E&I	Topsides	Safety	Process
With Construction	79	70	10	8	14598	1390	588	4840	2530	5250
In Backlog		9	2		2516	156	180	750	230	1200
In Progress (Unconstrained)	325	310	26	24	14075	4865	350	3680	1580	3600
In Progress (Constrained)										
Complete "A" Punches	206	200	20	18						
Fully Commissioned	41	36	29	20						
T.O. by Operations	38	33	20	18						
Growth Allowance					3599					
Additional Vendor Scope					3170	350	500	800	120	1400
NB Items Marked * (Specials)										
Totals	689	649	105	88	35442	6605	1438	9320	4230	10250

Illustration 8. Typical Weekly Score Card

Below is a typical Project Tracking Sheet

Project Tracking Sheet

System No.	System Description	Lead	System Total	Subsystem in work	Subsystem Complete	Estimated Man-hours	Additional Scope	Total hours achieved	Actual hours	P / F	% Complete	Non prod. Hours	Remaining hours	Weekly change
38	Glycol Regeneration	Proc.	1			220		220	0	#DIV/0!		0	220	47
39	Produced Water Treatment	Top.	2			500		500	0	#DIV/0!		0	500	0
39a	Oil Recalm / Slops Treatment	Mar.	1			240		240	240	-		0	0	0
40	Cooling Medium & Refrigeration	Mar.	2	2	2				0	#DIV/0!		0	0	0
41	Heating Medium	Top.	3	2		130		130	80	0,38	62 %	11	50	8
42	Chemical Handling	Top.	19	2	2	220	20	220	0	#DIV/0!		0	220	207
43	Flare, Ventilation & Blowdown	Top.	3	1	1	190		190	0	#DIV/0!		0	190	18
43a	Tanks Atmospheric Vents	Mar	2						0	#DIV/0!		0		0
45	Fuel Gas Condforing & Scrubbing	TBA	3			310		310	0	#DIV/0!		31	310	44
50	Seawater System Topside	Top.	4			110	40	110	0	#DIV/0!		82	110	-71
50a	Seawater System Vessel	Mar.	4	1	1	250		250	0	#DIV/0!		0	250	11
52	Hull Systems	Mar.	10	1	1	20		20	0	#DIV/0!		30	20	-385
52a	Turret & Bouy	Top.	2			500		500	0	#DIV/0!		0	500	0
53	Fresh Water	Mar.	4	3	3	222		222	0	#DIV/0!		16	222	285
55	Steam, Condesate & Hot Water	Mar.	5	1	1	20		20	0	#DIV/0!		0	20	15
56	Open Drains Vessel	Mar.	2	2	2	41	65	41	0	#DIV/0!		0	41	0
86	Key services Generation & Distribution	Mar.	2	2	2	230		230	0	#DIV/0!		0	230	60
88	Grounding and Lightning Protection	E & I	6	2	2	23		23	0	#DIV/0!		0	23	0
93	Telecomm Miscellaneous	E & I	3	1	1	945		945	212.2	1,02	22 %	78	733.116	
94	Navigation	E & I	7			421		421	149	0,40	35 %	21	272	
94a	Misc. Nav. Lights & Signals	E & I	1			1400		1400	42	0,67		10	1358	0
95	Enviromental & Metorological systems	E & I	1			130	25	130	100	1,22		44	30	0
96	Public Adress & General Alarm	E & I	7	1	1	210		210	80	0,75	38 %	21	130	274
97	Telecomm Power Supply	E & I	4	2	2	276		276	211	0,49		37	65	0
99	Comm. Events & Instr. Vendor	E & I	3			150		150	84	2,98	56 %	89	66	1,367
Temp	Temporary Systems	E & I	6	6	6	101		101	90	0,89	89 %	29	11	0
	Totals		468	109	84	31264		32314	5799	0,95	18 %	1951	26515	1283

Remaning total 385

Illustration 9. Typical Project Tracking Sheet

Below is a typical "Bean count" sheet

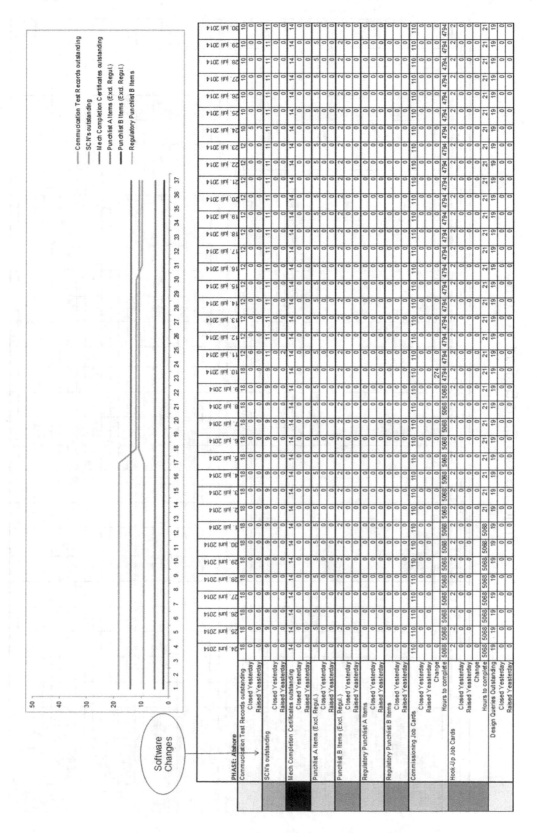

Illustration 10. Typical "Bean Count" sheet

Below is a typical Project scorecard by part system

Project Score Card By Part System

	Mechanical Completion				Handed to Commissioning				Commissioning Progress																Taken Over By Operations			
Sub-System		DCC		H / O Date		Sub-System		P/List		Sub-System		Scope Mhrs			%			F/C		Comm. Rec		R/list		B-Party	Dos	Sub-system		R/list
No	Description	Total	Done	Remaining	Plan	Actual	No	Description	A	B	No	Description	Plan	Actual	Remain	Plan	Act	No	Remain	Parts	O/std	A	B	B	%	No	Description	B
4.03.01	W/ Shops on Main Deck Fwd																											
4.04.01	T/Hole Mech. Handling Equip																											
4.04.02	Aft Thruster Lifting Device																											
4.04.03	Fwd Thruster Lifting Device																											
4.04.04	I-Beam/Trolley Aft. Space																											
4.04.05	I-Beam/Trolley Fwd. Space																											
4.04.10	Forward Crane																											
4.04.20	Midships Crane																											
4.04.30	Aft Crane																											
6.04.50	Turret Mech. Handling Equip																											
4.05.01	Turret Closing Plate M/Pool																											
4.05.10	Moorings, Piles, Buoy Struct																											
4.05.20	Spider Buoy																											
4.06.01	Thruster Control Equip. CCR																											
4.06.10	Thruster No. 1 Aft Center																											
4.06.11	Thruster No. 2 Aft Port																											
4.06.12	Thruster No. 3 Aft Stbd																											
4.06.20	Thruster No. 4 Fwd Aft End																											
4.06.21	Thruster No. 5 Fwd/Fore End																											
4.06.50	Hatch Cover NP - 06310 (Aft)																											
4.06.51	Hatch Cover NP - 06320 (Aft)																											
4.06.52	Hatch Cover NP - 06330 (Aft)																											
4.06.53	Hatch Cover NP - 06340 (Aft)																											
4.06.54	Hatch Cover NP - 06350 (Fw)																											
4.06.90	Manoeuvring and Sea Trials																											
4.07.01	Ships Area Completion																											
4.07.02	Module M02/Water Injection																											
3.07.03	Module M03 - Sep. HP Comp.																											
3.07.04	Module M04 - Sep. Glycol																											
3.07.05	Module M05 - Sep. LP. Comp																											
4.07.08	Flare																											
2.07.09	Module M09 - Generation																											
3.08.01	Lube Oil																											
4.08.02	Portable Cargo Monitoring																											
2.09.01	Aft Impressed Current Cont.																											
2.09.02	Fwd Impressed Current Cont.																											
6.16.01	Leak Recovery System																											
6.16.02	Swivel Lubrication																											
6.16.03	Fluid Buffer System																											
6.16.09	Lower Turret Structure																											
6.19.90	Turret Structure - Bull Arm																											
6.19.91	Spider Buoy																											
7.18.01	Glory Hole NW																											
7.18.02	Glory Hole SW																											
7.18.03	Glory Hole NE																											
7.18.04	Glory Hole SE																											
8.04.01	Host 'A' M/Fold, F/Lines, Riser																											
8.03.10	Xmas Tree HPGI (HA-S1)																											
8.03.11	Xmas Tree SS (HA-S2)																											
8.03.12	Xmas Tree HPGI (HA-S3)																											
8.03.13	Xmas Tree HPGS (HA-S4)																											
8.04.02	Host 'B' M/Fold, F/Lines, Riser																											

Illustration 11. Typical Project Scorecard by part system

Below is a typical Vendor tracking sheet

Vendor Tracking Sheet

System	Description	Lead	Vendor	Prty.	Planned Mhrs	Growth Hours	Mhrs Forecast	Earned Mhrs E	Actual Mhrs E	Prod.	% Comp	Non Prod	Man-hours to go	Week Change
0	Temporary Systems	All.			270		270	270	279	1,03	100,0 %		0	0
4	Lifting Systems	Mar.	Liebeah		820		820	100	100	1,00	12,2 %		720	0
6	Thrusters	Mar.	RR/ Simrad/ABB							#DIV/0!	#DIV/0!		0	0
8	Auxiliary Vessel Systems	Mar.	Various							#DIV/0!	#DIV/0!		0	0
9	Corrosion Protection and Marking	Mar.	Century							#DIV/0!	#DIV/0!		0	0
16	Turret Systems	Top.	FMC		600		600	600	0	0	#DIV/0!	0,0 %		600	0
18	Subsea (23 Future) (11 Offshore)	OAD	Kongsberg		720		720	81	209	2,58	11,3 %		639	0
20	Separation and Stabilisation (1 Future)	Pro.	BJ Process		300		300	0	0	#DIV/0!	0,0 %		300	0
21	Crude Handling	Pro.	BJ Process		1410		1410	0	0	#DIV/0!	0,0 %		1410	0
22	Crude Oil Metering & Re-Circulation	Pro.	BJ Process		300		300	0	0	#DIV/0!	0,0 %		300	0
23	Gas Compression & Re-Injection to Reservoir	Pro.	Nuovo Pign.		4260		4260	400	240	0,60	9,4 %		3860	0
24	Gas Drying and Cooling	Pro.	Reid		160		160	160	0	#DIV/0!	0,0 %		160	0
29	Water Injection (2 Future)	Mar.	Weir Pumps		200		200	200	0	#DIV/0!	0,0 %		200	0
31	Oil Storage and Import	Mar.	Daniel							#DIV/0!	#DIV/0!		0	0
32	Ship Offloading	Pro.	Daniel/Hitec							#DIV/0!	#DIV/0!		0	0
38	Glycol Regeneration	Top.	Reid		200		200	200	0	#DIV/0!	0,0 %		200	0
39	Produced Water Treatment or Reclaimed oil	Top.	Kent		70		70	70	0	#DIV/0!	0,0 %		70	0
41	Heating Medium	Top.	ABB		210		210	210	0	#DIV/0!	0,0 %		210	0
42	Chemical Handling	Top.	CDS		884		884	884	0	#DIV/0!	0,0 %		884	0
43	Flare Ventilation and Blowdown	Top.	Zinc		1200		1200	1200	0	#DIV/0!	0,0 %		1200	0
45	Fuel Gas Conditioning & Scrubbing	Pro.	Reid		180		180	180	0	#DIV/0!	0,0 %		180	0
50	Seawater System Topside	Top.	Weir Pumps		240		240	240	0	#DIV/0!	0,0 %		240	0
52a	Turret & Buoy	Top.	FMC		240		240	240	0	#DIV/0!	0,0 %		240	0
58	Turret Hydraulic Power (Water Based)	Top.	OSI		420		420	420	0	#DIV/0!	0 %		420	0

Illustration 12. Typical Vendor tracking sheet

Below is a typical Leads Individual performance Reports

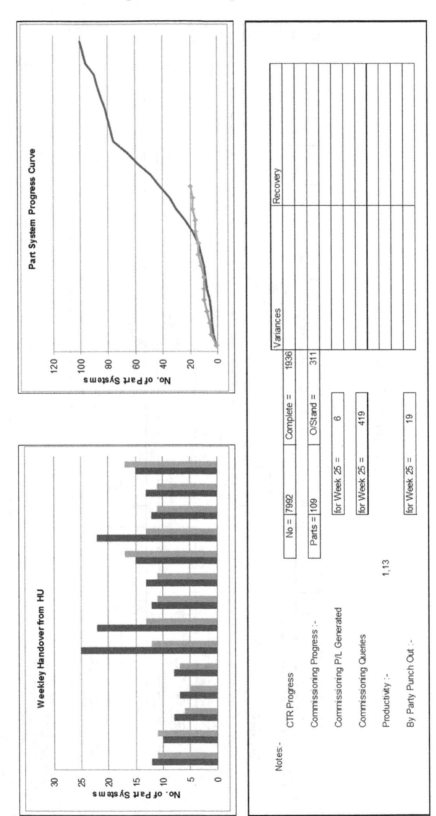

Illustration 13. Typical Leads Individual performance Report

What to do when the systems fails.

In addition to making sure you have a report structure in place, you need to have a way around system failures so you can still monitor and control the job if the database breaks down for shorter or longer periods.

To avoid the delays that will occur when the progress roll-up has the misfortune to fail, the following guidelines should be implemented:

a) On a weekly basis after the normal progress routine has been completed; make a copy of the progress statement for the networking dataset. This copy should contain the activity number, the lead responsible engineer, a short description for reference purpose, percentage complete, man-hours and weekly date format.

b) Select the appropriate data system to cover your needs whether it is an Access or Excel set up. As said prior to this; "keep it simple", you do not want to design such a complex system that it takes more time to operate than the original system that failed.

c) Once the system has been designed, it should only take the skills of a technical clerk to keep it updated.

Below is a typical manual report

Typical Manual (easy to use - if the system - fails) Report

Lead	Activity	Activity Description	Planned	Remain	Actual	% Date 24.06.2014	Achieved 2014	01.07.14	08.07.14	15.07.14	22.07.14	29.07.14	05.08.14	12.08.14	19.08.14	26.08.14
BS	COC10020HV	CommissionTemp. Power Supply to ES-90001	200	-83	283	100 %	200	20								
bs1	COC10020	Electrical STR (00.20)	271	271	0	100 %	271									
BS	COC10020M1	Temporary Power Supply to M01 (ES-82601)	20	0	20	100 %	20				3					
BS	COC10020M3	Temporary Power Supply to M03 (ES-82003)	60	-40	100	100 %	60									
BS	COC10020M5	Temporary Power Supply to M05 (ES-82004)	60	0	60	100 %	60		2							
BS	COC10020M9	Temp. Power Supply to M09 (ES-80101/80201)	60	0	60	100 %	60				15					
BS	COC10020UP	Commission Temp. UPS supply to Turret	40	0	40	100 %	40									
	0020	Temporary Power System	711	148	563		711									
WW	COC10030	Commn. Temp. Firewater System	90	90	0	100 %	90									
WW	COC10030A	Install Valve in Temp. F/W Line	40	22	18		0									
ww1	COP10030	Piping CTR (00.30)	20	20	0	100 %	20									
ww1	COX10030	Mechanical CTR (00.30)	0	0	0	100 %	0					8				
WW	COC10030X	Complete Commn. Punchlist for 00.30	20	12	8	100 %	20									
	0030	Temporary Firewater System	170	144	26		130									
WW	COC10040	Commn. Temp. Firewater Pumps	420	420	0		0									
ww1	COX10040	Mechanical CTR (00.40)	0	0	0		0						2			
	0040	Temporary Firewater Pumps	420	420	0		0									
AA	COC10301	Workshop Labs & Stores	40	40	0		0									
aa1	COW10301	Electrical CTR (03.01)	26	26	0		0							2		
aa1	COX10301	Mechanical CTR (03.01)	0	0	0		0									
AA	COC10301X	Complete Commn. Punchlist for 03.01	60	52	8	100 %	60									
	03	Workshop Labs & Stores	126	118	8		60									

Dynamic Commissioning Hours

Illustration 14. Typical manual report

Defining the Work Scope and Building the Schedule

Defining the Work Scope - Sequence of Events

Define the Commissioning Packages first, then the MC packs.

Once you have defined the Commissioning Packages and marked them up on a set of Master P&ID's (1), Construction can now identify the smaller work scope. This constitute the Mechanical Completion Packages (MC packs) (2) within the boundaries of the Commissioning Packages. The associated tags (3) can then be identified and the Work Orders (4) developed for fabrication.

All this data is subsequently ready to be stored in the Project Completion System database (PCS, PCD or other fancy acronyms).

The illustration below shows the sequence in which the various work elements of the job need to be defined: Namely that Commissioning packs are the drivers for the definition of the construction work, and that the commissioning activities are the drivers for the sequence of construction work. This is however only true after all heavy components and major piping have been installed.

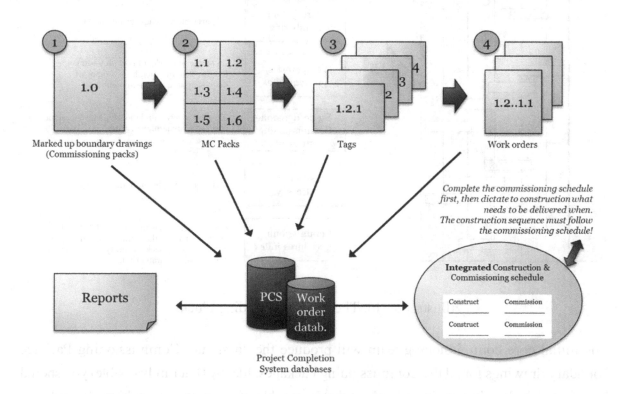

Illustration 15. Defining work scope- sequence of events

Building the Schedule

Assuming you have got all your boundary drawings marked up to define the commissioning packages and you have numbered them all, you are ready to start putting everything together in one integrated schedule.

Now, let's pause for a minute and ask ourselves a question before we continue:

What are the major elements and philosophies we need to consider and have in place before the work to build the schedule can start?

The illustration below shows the necessary building block that you must have ready before you start.

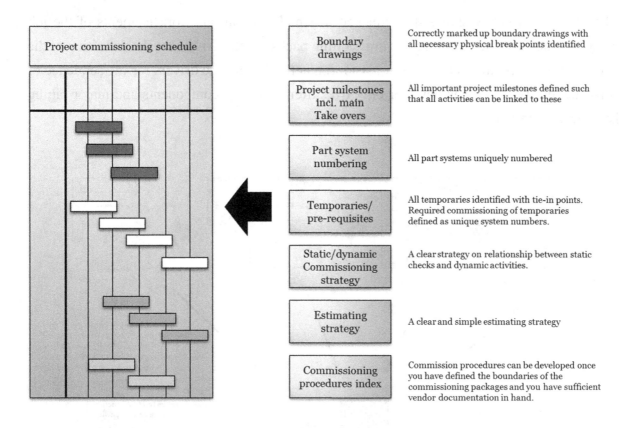

Boundary drawings	Correctly marked up boundary drawings with all necessary physical break points identified
Project milestones incl. main Take overs	All important project milestones defined such that all activities can be linked to these
Part system numbering	All part systems uniquely numbered
Temporaries/ pre-requisites	All temporaries identified with tie-in points. Required commissioning of temporaries defined as unique system numbers.
Static/dynamic Commissioning strategy	A clear strategy on relationship between static checks and dynamic activities.
Estimating strategy	A clear and simple estimating strategy
Commissioning procedures index	Commission procedures can be developed once you have defined the boundaries of the commissioning packages and you have sufficient vendor documentation in hand.

Illustration 16. The schedule building blocks

The initial core commissioning team will produce the "first-cut" Commissioning Package boundary drawings for all the Commissioning Packages. Ideally (but rarely doable) you should have a senior planning engineer in place that is capable of doing this work himself, and then when the senior commissioning engineers are recruited they have a good starting point to work from.

The packages will be marked up utilizing P&ID's, electrical single line diagrams, Plot plans and Control arrangements. The numbered packages then form the basis for the Commissioning Network. Pre-requisites listings by systems will be produced which in turn help define any requirements for temporary facilities, installation of valves or breaks etc. required for an efficient commissioning, as well as the logic in the network and the agreed milestones and priorities.

With the following pieces in place, the commissioning plan can be produced:

- Project Planning tool in place
- Agreed and defined Milestones and Priorities
- Agreed Duration's for the commissioning activities
- Commissioning Boundaries complete and numbered
- Pre-requisites/Temporaries lists complete

Once the plan is in place, a budget estimate can be provided along with all the required suites of reports.

The marked up drawing should then be filed into the Commissioning Dossiers (basis for the hand-over dossier, later described), and any additional or supplementary information relevant to the specific commissioning package should be stored herein. (See Documentation section 4.0)

The durations for each activity will initially be determined by the commissioning manager and the senior planner based on their expertise and years of experience. Later these durations will be refined by the commissioning engineer through the formal estimating process.

Once the durations are in place, a budget estimate can be produced from the manpower histograms and commissioning team requirements.

Don't underestimate the time it takes to develop the 'first cut' schedule and budget estimate.

Typically this is a 3 months job.

The diagram below shows the basic sequence of events in building the schedule

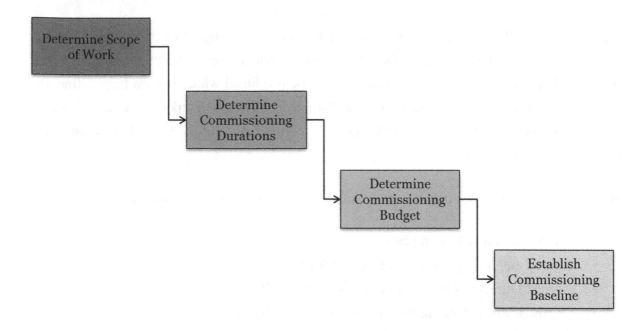

Illustration 17. Building the schedule. Sequence of events

Commissioning Schedule Development

(The "Input-Process-Output" Chart)

The illustration below depicts the Inputs, the Processes, the Outputs and the respective responsible parties in the development of the initial Commissioning Schedule.

Note: The illustration does not reflect the work required to integrate the Commissioning and Construction schedule. This is covered later in this section.

INPUTS			PROCESSES			OUTPUTS	
What	**Who**		**What**	**Who**		**What**	**From Whom**
1) Company milestones and Philosophies	Owners		Set as fixed points in schedule	Planner			
2) Boundary drawings	Senior Commissioning Engineers/Planner		Develop detail commissioning procedures	Senior Commissioning Engineers/ Planner			
3) Part system numbering	Planner (coding manual)		Set as part system numbers in Commissioning schedule	Planner			• Owners
4) Prerequisite listing	Planner/Senior Commissioning Engineers		Build into commissioning procedures and schedule	Senior Commissioning Engineers/ Planner			• Construction Management • Commissioning Leads/Engineers
5) Commissioning procedures list	Senior Commissioning Engineers		Align with part systems coding and develop procedures completion schedule	Planner			• Engineering Management • Project Management
6) Temporary requirements	Senior Commissioning Engineers		Build into commissioning procedures and schedule	Senior Commissioning Engineers/ Planner			
7) Estimating strategy	Planner/ Commissioning Manager		Develop durations and manpower requirements	Senior Commissioning Engineers/ Planner			

Output column (rotated labels): 1) Commissioning Schedule 2) Design prerequisites 3) Commissioning procedures completion schedule 4) Commissioning budget

Illustration 18. The schedule input-process-output chart

Building the Schedule – Critical Ground Rules

In order to build a realistic schedule you have to make sure that all elements that take up time and resources or are needed for schedule-control, are adequately captured and reflected in the schedule. In this way you will avoid some of the unnecessary and time-consuming schedule revisions later in the game.

The illustration below shows the elements that in addition to the "standard commissioning activities" must be remembered and implemented when building the initial schedule, and should form part of your ground rules for building a quality schedule.

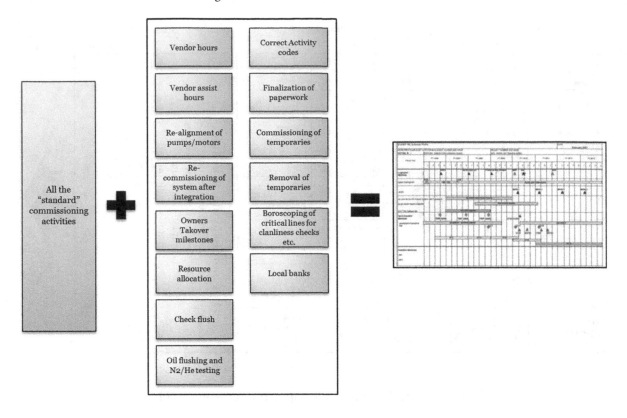

Illustration 19. Critical ground rules

Critical Ground Rules

These are the descriptions of the critical elements and ground rules identified on the previous page.

• *Always build the vendor hours and vendor assistance hours into the schedule*

If vendors are assumed to do actual work that will show up as progress (which of course they will), always build the vendor estimate into the schedule. In this way you control ALL work, and ALL work necessary to complete the job is actually reflected in the overall project schedule. Still some contractors, as well as operators, for mysterious reasons don't do this and hence have a very hard time explaining where the hours go and great difficulties in maintaining a timely vendor attendance built on the timing of activities reflected in the plan. In addition, the vendors will require manpower assistance, so make sure you build this in as well! Make sure that you have sufficient expertise/equipment available on site for doing analysis following your flushing, N2/He leak testing, and retro jetting, etc.

- *Always build in allowance for re-alignment of pumps/compressors, etc.*

If your project is a typical modular concept where modules are built separately and later integrated into one large platform, you might as well make sure you have sufficient allowance built in for re-alignment work. No matter what your designers or less experienced commissioning engineers tell you, deck deflections due to shifting weight forces when modules are lifted, draft variances and inadequate lifting gear ALWAYS change the alignment and / or give additional stress on nozzles and pipes.

- *Always allow for sufficient re-commissioning of systems at the integration site*

If you have commissioned part of a system at the module yard, say the steam boiler and the module distribution network, you will have to re-commission these when you have hooked up the other modules at the integration site. Only then will you be able to test the system with something that resembles full load. This goes for most of the utility systems like air, freshwater, firewater, main power distribution etc. Again and again, we see projects that simply forget to allow for this in the schedule and hence suffer the consequences.

- *Always build the company's goals / milestones into the schedule*

The basis for the commissioning plan will be the agreed Milestones based on company created requirements. If each activity or event is related to a Milestone from the outset of the plan, then only improvements to the plan will be made. Once created and agreed all changes should be monitored and registered on a Schedule Change Request form. (SCR)

- *Always build the major Take Over packages into the schedule*

The major Take Over packages, sometimes referred to as *the ultimate KPIs* should be defined as project milestones. This is probably the most effective tool to ensure focus from the *whole* project team toward the main deliverable, namely the owners requirements represented by taken over systems.

- *Always allow for the correct resources*

Once the activities are created, the correct 'use' of resources needs to be applied. As commissioning activities will not be specific disciplines alone, a mixture of process, mechanical, instrument, electrical and piping will be needed. This really needs to be thought through when developing the basic estimates. However it is not until the procedures are written that a full understanding of the complete scope is evident. It is important at an early stage that the senior planner and the core team take a thorough review of the basic estimate to make sure the full resource make up is accounted for. Very often you will find that the responsible engineer looks at the boundary drawing and simply forgets to account for all the disciplines needed.

- *Always allow time for pre-acceptance from Construction and check-flush prior to filling the systems*

This will ensure that you have built in time to satisfy yourself that you start out with a clean system.

- *Always build in time for the oil flushing and N2/He-leak-testing*

Obviously you always build this in. However, what we see time and time again, especially for oil flushing is that the estimates are always too low. Unless you have a hands-on expert to do the estimate; double them!! Always include expert companies to carry out this work.

Prior to commissioning of the gas systems build in allowance for the N2/He leak testing to ensure you have a gas tight system.

- *Always create appropriate sort codes*

These activity codes are probably the most important part of the schedule. The correct codes will allow for sorting and are the basis for all required reports; by system/part system, by lead engineer, by takeover package, by vendor etc.

- *Always allow sufficient time to finalize the paperwork*

When you include activities for the pre-commissioning tests, using dedicated test sheets (which you normally will), allow sufficient time in the schedule to finalize the paperwork. The same goes for preparing the paperwork before handover to Operations. This is a time consuming activity constantly underestimated; hence your progress suffers if these activities don't show up on the plan as part of the normal commissioning activity duration.

- *Always allow time in the schedule for commissioning of and removal of temporaries*

Again a much overlooked activity. Temporary equipment often is required to be commissioned before it can be put into service and that takes time. Likewise it takes time to remove temporary equipment. Make sure this is reflected in the schedule.

- *Always build in allowance for boroscoping*

Experience tells us that systems handed over from construction to commissioning generally have 'lost' preservation cover, and you want to make absolutely certain that you've got a clean system. Typical critical systems to boroscope are gas compression, gas handling, water injection and separation.

- *Always include load bank facilities for Main Power Generator testing*

You cannot commission all systems the same time as you commission your main power generators. You will seldom have enough load to adequately perform your generator testing / power management testing while relying on the main power generators to deliver load to support the commissioning of other equipment and systems simultaneously. So make sure you build in allowance for the load banks.

Load banks are expensive rental equipment, so you need to make sure the timing is correct to avoid too much stand-by time.

The best concept cost and schedule wise, is to include load bank testing to take place at the suppliers work or / and at the module yard.

- *Evaluate the need for inclusion of allowance for "hidden/unrevealed" work*

Based on audits at the various module yards and growth rate at these, you should include a portion for "hidden/unrevealed" work at the integration site. It is not unusual to see this category in the range of 10-30% (!).

Commissioning Boundary Drawings

Probably the single most important element of the up-front commissioning work in the engineering phase of the project is to define the correct boundaries for your commissioning packages.

Here you have a significant potential for failures!

Remember, the definition of these packages is going to dictate how you will commission the systems, in what sequence, how the part systems are numbered, how your procedures are written and how everything will be logically linked in your plan. It will even dictate necessary engineering changes to facilitate an effective commissioning.

The importance of getting these done right from the start cannot be emphasized enough.

A very important prerequisite in getting these right is of course that your basis is a well advanced set of engineering drawings such as P&IDs, electrical single line diagrams and control arrangements.

The 'event / effect-diagram' below shows the potential risks of incorrect mark-up of the commissioning boundary drawings.

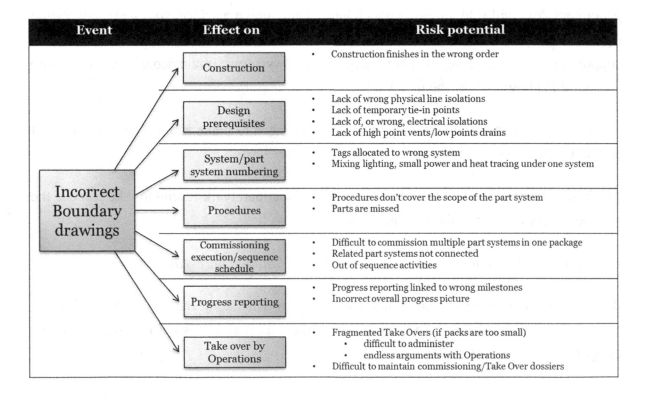

Illustration 20. Event/effect diagram, incorrect boundary drawings

Commissioning Boundary Drawings Do's and Don'ts

The sketch below is a real life example and shows a very typical mistake (dark gray box-*No*) in determining package boundaries, and the correct way of doing it (light gray box-*Yes*).

Note: This is not to say that work cannot start on the single pump and valves but don't try to hand over this small unit to Operations.

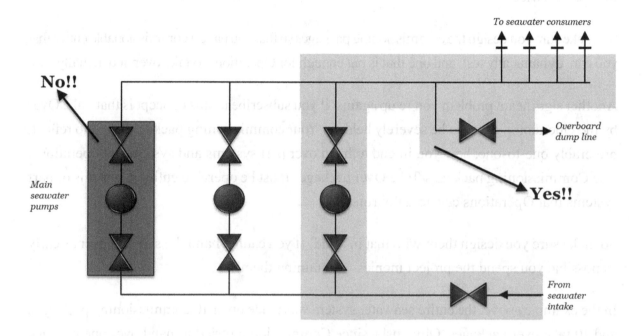

Illustration 21. Example of wrong and right marked up boundary drawing (principle)

So what's wrong? Surely you can commission the motor. You can do your 4 hour uncoupled run. You can turn the pump (if it is small enough), and you can commission the suction and discharge valves.

Of course you can, but where is that going to take you?

You don't have a system that you can dynamically run! What's commissioning all about?

Yes! Systems, systems and system, *NOT* disciplines.

In this example, you don't have a system, or part system that you can run. You only have static parts. Therefore, the system will have to be tested again once all parts of it are complete (with the exception of the 4 hour run). So, the progress you earned up front was really no progress at all. Most likely, it was negative progress for the project as you will have to go back and test everything later.

There is actually a name for this bits-and-pieces approach; it is called *commissioning by basic functions.*

Some contractor companies, even large ones have this approach built into their philosophy and strategy documents, and their clients don't even question it! With this strategy you pay for the job twice!

So, make sure you design the commissioning packages so that you have a commissionable entity that you can, dynamically test, and one that is big enough for Operations to take over and actually run.

Another significant problem you're up against if you subscribe to this concept is that Take Over by the Operator is going to be severely held up. Your commissioning packages need to reflect, preferably one-to-one, how you intend to hand over part systems and systems to Operations. The Commissioning packages/Take Over packages must be operable entities, systems or part systems that Operations can actually run.

So make sure you design them with that in mind! If you cannot hand the systems over as early as possible you spend the project monies maintaining them!

In the example above, the entire seawater system was made up of 10 commissioning packages, and 10 take over packages. Obviously, since Commissioning tried to hand over one package (one motor, one pump and two valves) Operations turned around and said, "Come back another day when you have something sensible for us to run."

Another very important element of the boundary drawings discussions:

Make sure that you don't mix commissioning packages on the same drawing. You want *unique drawings* for each commissioning package. Then there is no confusion where the packages start and finish, no confusion relative to what is covered in the associated procedure and no doubt as to what you will hand over to Operations. You are accountable for the correct definition of the commissioning packages, but it always pays to have Operations take a quick review to ensure alignment with the Take Over Philosophy.

The illustrations below show how confusing the picture gets when you have more than one commissioning package on one drawing, and the room it creates for errors.

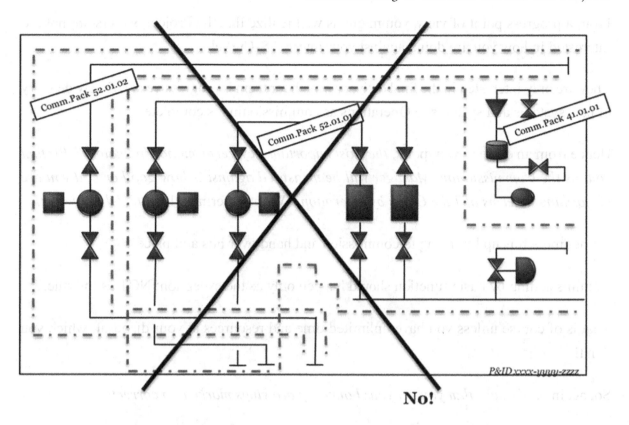

No!

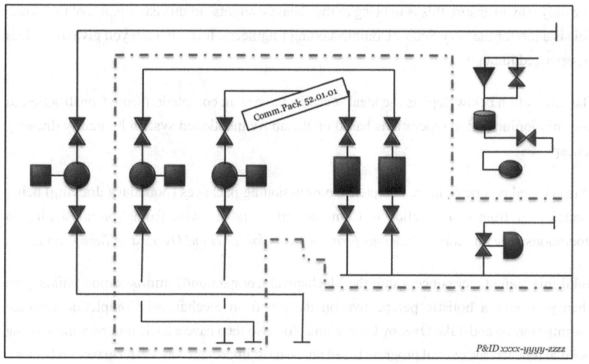

Yes!

Illustration 22. Example of wrong and right marked up boundary drawing.

From a progress point of view, you might as well realize that the Project owners are not too interested in how you are doing against your internal S-Curve!

They are only interested in the final delivery, which for them is progressive and timely delivery of part systems and systems to Operations as commissioning is complete.

Hence from an owner's viewpoint, *the most important Key Performance Indicator (KPI) that you, as the Commissioning Manager will be measured against is how good or bad you are performing in terms of Take Overs by Operations.* We have termed this; *the Ultimate KPI.*

Do not mess this up by trying to commission and hand over bits and pieces!

Commissioning by basic function should happen only as the exception; NOT as the rule.

That is of course unless you have unlimited time and resources at your disposal, which you don't!

So, again; *make sure that you get your boundary drawings marked up correctly.*

The only way to ensure this is to bring in the "heavy-weights" in this early phase of the game. This is a job for the very Senior Commissioning Engineers. It is not a job you give to the less experienced juniors!

The illustration below depicts the ideal scenario for system completion from Construction to Commissioning and to Operations based on the above mentioned system boundary drawing concept.

This is based on one or more complete Commissioning packages (boundary drawing) being handed over from Construction to Commissioning and likewise from Commissioning to Operations. *The boundary drawings form the basis for all Hand Overs and Take Overs!*

Build this Hand Over concept into the Mechanical Completion/Commissioning philosophy. Then you have a holistic perspective on the job from mechanical Completion through Commissioning and Take Over by Operations. You also then have a basic progress-monitoring tool that reflects true overall progress based on the most important Key Performance Indicators.

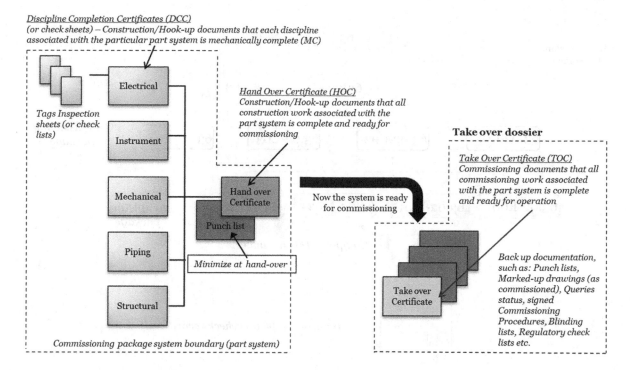

Illustration 23. Ideal scenario for system completion from
Construction to Commissioning and to Operations.

Part System Numbering

It is essential that once you have your boundary drawings marked up, you must ensure that you follow a unique numbering system in line with the project's coding manual. There must be NO interfaces that slip between the cracks, so that each commissioning package reflects the exact limits of the boundary drawings, and is uniquely numbered.

Below is a typical system breakdown structure

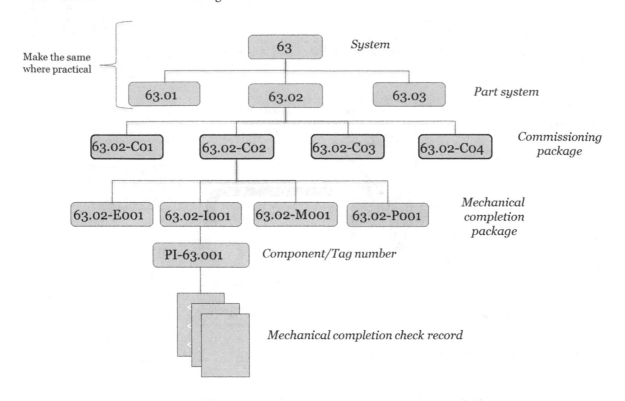

Illustration 24. Typical system breakdown structure

Note: The challenge is not to number the commissioning packages, but to make sure that the right boundary limits are identified and correctly allocated.

Temporaries

All the temporary equipment you'll require to commission your project must be identified and uniquely numbered. For example;

- At the module yard you want to commission the seawater distribution network in the module, but the main seawater pumps sit in a different module at a different yard. Then you will need a temporary seawater pump.

- You may want to commission your level transmitters via the distributed control system, but you don't have a user interface -an operator station. Then you'll need a temporary one to help you out.

- You want to flush your hydraulic distribution system as early as possible, but the main pump and filters are in a different module. Then you will need to mobilize a temporary flushing unit. When the whole system comes together at a later stage, you will use the main pump and filters as a check flush.

- You would possibly also like to commission the deluge system as early as possible to determine gaps in coverage. Then you would need a temporary pump sized for the specific capacity and later at the integration site you will re-run the test with the main fire water pumps.

Make sure you have identified all the required temporaries and marked up on your boundary drawing where you intend to tie them in to the permanent systems.

Where necessary, *make sure you identify activities in the plan for commissioning of the temporaries, and again number these uniquely.* An easy way to number temporaries is to use one system number for all these and then, subdivide this number for the various temporary activities.

Do not try to number the temporaries with the same numbers as the systems to which they are tied in. That only creates unnecessary confusion!

And, of course some of these temporaries will have to be removed/"de-commissioned", and as long as these activities will require commissioning manpower, than YES; include those activities in the plan!

Static/Dynamic Commissioning Strategy

As you know, most dynamic commissioning activities are preceded by static pre-checks, sometimes called CP's (commissioning pre-checks), FTC's (function test certificates), PCC (pre-commissioning checks) or other fancy names and acronyms that all mean the same;

Static checks (except of course motor runs, which by nature are dynamic) and must be performed prior to the dynamic activities.

Before you build the schedule you must have a clear philosophy in place on how you want to perform these checks, or more importantly WHEN you want these checks done.

Do you want these done as early as possible (e.g. at the module yards), or do you want to wait until you have a more integrated unit to work with? Maybe you want something in between these two options. Regardless of how much commissioning you complete early, you'll still have a last check to do when all the modules come together.

It all depends on the configuration and geographical nature of your project. Regardless of configuration and geography variations, or if you should expect significant time lag between static checks and the start of dynamics, there is one rule you should always try to live by:

Maximize close-linking of static pre-checks and dynamic commissioning

Why?

Although it can be advantageous to get your commissioning team going early, especially seen from a project/equipment familiarization viewpoint, you have to carefully weigh the advantages against the disadvantages.

There is actually only one advantage, and that is the familiarization with the equipment.

One can argue that to detect deficiencies early is an advantage, but from an overall project perspective this very often tends to delay the schedule rather than improve on it. Analysis of hours spent on a number of large projects support this argument.

The reasons are threefold:

- Firstly to have Commissioning stepping on Construction's toes while they are trying to construct the unit is often very inefficient and can easily create irritation and complaints from both parties. You, as the manager don't have time to waste on such problems.
- Secondly, you will be frequently hit with engineering changes in this phase of the game and as a result chances are that you will have to repeat your pre-checks over again.
- Thirdly, there is a significant safety element involved. Say you do your pre-checks at a module yard and integration of modules takes place 3-6 months after you have completed the checks. Would you trust that nothing has happened during that period to change your recorded and documented settings on the particular equipment? Will you be willing to start the dynamic activities without checking the status again?

Even though most projects have rigorous Permit to Work systems in place, there are numerous examples out there that describe nasty incidents attributed to equipment status changing from early module yard days to integration time.

We are not saying that you shouldn't do pre-checks at module yards, but merely that you need to consider the risks from both a schedule impact and safety perspective in terms of how early you do them. From a philosophy viewpoint *you should do your pre-checks as close to the dynamics as practically possible.* This is what we call *"close-linking"* of activities. Variations should be treated as exceptions and evaluated on a, case-by-case basis.

The illustration below depicts this concept.

Maximize close-linking of static pre-checks and dynamic commissioning

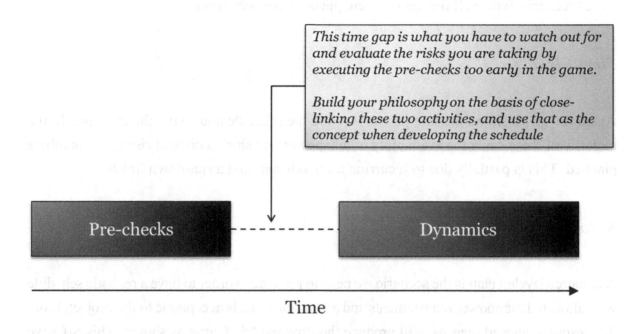

This time gap is what you have to watch out for and evaluate the risks you are taking by executing the pre-checks too early in the game.

Build your philosophy on the basis of close-linking these two activities, and use that as the concept when developing the schedule

Pre-checks

Dynamics

Time

Illustration 25. Close-linking of pre-checks and dynamics

Planning and Planning Considerations

Developing the Project Plan

Once you are satisfied with the basic schedule, i.e. the "time related" plan with durations, first pass man-hours, and an expected completion date, you should look at the resources that are required and available to complete the project. Remember; people, equipment, material and money do the work, so make sure you have enough when you need them. Add the resources into your plan, run the histograms and you will see at an instant if your levels are out of synch with the time analyses. This is the time for the tradeoff. Could you deliver the unit sooner if you had more resources, more money, or is it physically impossible to get that amount of labor in one area? All of these points should be discussed and checked with the project team prior to refining the schedule. When agreed, the team can complete the schedule, time based and resource leveled.

Time Analysis Only

You can see from the graph on the next page, the initial effects of a time run analysis where the profile for the number of men required is very erratic. This run is also derived from a "total logic" scenario, where all the known prerequisites have been input.

Time Fixed

Again the graph shows the first pass at leveling the schedule and fixing the end date. In the majority of these cases the availability of manpower will show a distinct rise in the numbers planned. This is partially due to incurring a smooth start and a run-down finish.

Resource Leveled

A resource leveled plan is the scenario we need to produce in order to have a realistic schedule with allocated manpower requirements and an end date that is acceptable to the project. From this resource leveled plan we will produce the Progress "S" Curve as shown. This S-Curve will be aggressive at the start of the project, to keep the pressure on.

All schedules given to your Lead Engineers to progress and complete the scope will be based on the Early Start details. Performance reports, time now analysis reports and Lead engineers reports, should also be produced based on the Early Start scenario.

Back Up and History

In almost every Project there is never sufficient back-up of data, and the historic knowledge created to provide final documentation and certainly not enough to cover potential insurance claims.

Having to go back, reload data, examine for the details to prove the point is costly and time consuming.

See illustrations below.

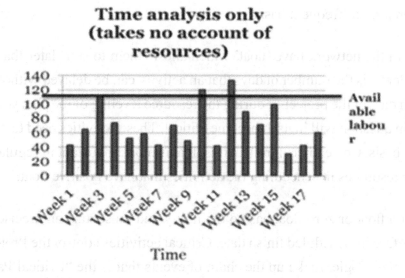

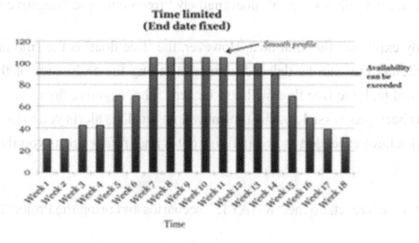

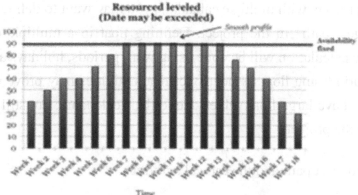

Illustration 26. Time Analysis/Time Limited/Resourced leveled histograms

Critical Path

The most important part of your plan is the 'Critical Path." This must be monitored at least on a weekly basis, however it becomes apparent that time will dictate whether or not to monitor the critical path on a more frequent basis.

Certain activities in the network have 'float' which allows them to start later than their early dates. The "total float," is the number of days that an activity can be delayed without having an effect on the finish date of the project. If during the resource leveling of the plan you use up this float, the activity in question will in itself become critical. These activities need to be monitored on a case-by-case basis. Correctly controlled, this float is most important in regulating the use of labor and other resources in scheduling the activities that have positive float.

An activity with no float or zero float has no flexibility and must start on precisely that date and finish on or before its scheduled finish date. Critical activities control the Project duration and together with their logic, make up the chain of events that is the "Critical Path." Within your plan there are two other kinds of 'float' namely "free float" and "negative float."

We have already explained the total float. However, the 'free float' is the amount of time the early start of the activity can be delayed without delaying the early start of the successor. Within the critical path the free float will also be zero. The 'negative float' will happen after the network has been progressed and the time now date set. This alerts you to the fact that one or more activities have exceeded their late finish dates and in fact warns you that the Project is delayed.

This is when you must react, do the "WHAT IF" scenarios and bring the Project back on time.

Be advised that in projects with multiple calendars, you may want to define critical activities based on the "longest path" in the project. Defining float in a multiple calendar is more complicated and the calculation will be done using work periods, holidays and any exception built into the network. Using float to identify critical activities may prove misleading, since some activities may have large float values due to their calendars, but still be critical to the completion date on the project.

Always assess the longest path and the critical activities.

The illustration on the next page shows a typical critical path

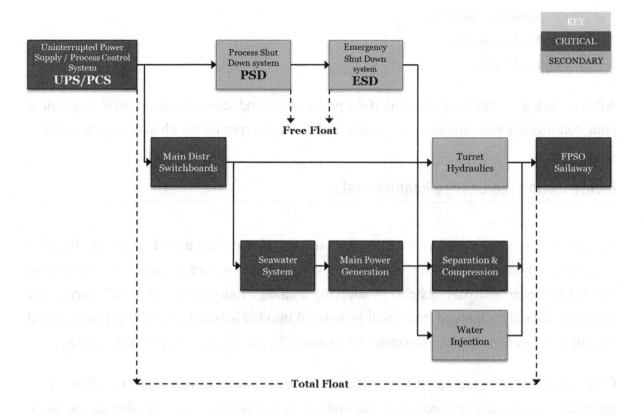

Illustration 27. Critical path scenario
(Typical, for illustration purposes only)

Timing and Updating of the Plan

Updating the plan on a regular basis becomes very important because even the most detailed plan will fail unless it is monitored on a regular cycle. Simplify the process by coding activities in such a way that will allow selective activities to be withdrawn from the schedule. Up-front results will streamline the process and keep you up-to-date on how the project is progressing.

The following sequence is a guide to adjust and glean information from your plan:

1) Schedule the project and run reports series.
2) Compare reported progress to the original plan.
3) Level resources (at time now, the bow wave effect will happen if reported progress is less than planned).
4) Weekly adjustments (at time now).
   • Maintain date

- Maintain resources
- Analyze results

5) Adjust the Plan

After updating and leveling the plan, if the project is behind schedule you, need to implement your contingency plan and or adapt your schedule to incorporate the change requirements.

Incorporating the Change Requirements

As per the 'timing and updating of the plan' section, all incorporated changes into the plan must be strictly monitored. The charts on the following pages show a sample of how to monitor by lead engineer and part system. In adopting a change monitoring system all parties are involved and only approved items will be entered into the schedule. This also gives a good insight into future potential insurance claims made, by, company, contractor or vendor.

Consolidated into the actual "Change Request" sheet is the schedule impact section where the planning engineer will conclude the findings of the analysis once the change and logic have been input into the network. Only major unavoidable impacts will be duly signed and approved by the next management level up.

Remember to COMMUNICATE this information to all concerned!

Below are typical versions of Schedule Change Request form and Schedule Change Request register.

Commissioning Schedule Change Request

	Commissioning Schedule Change Request		No. CS Sheet.	
Discipline	Part System No	Job Card No.	Date	
To:	From	Position Lead		

Proposed Change:

Proposed Implemented Change :

	New Activity			
	Changed Duration			
	Changed Man-hour			
	Logic Changes			
	Other Additions			

| | Signed : | |
| | Date | |

Schedule Revision NO ... ...   Input into Revision NO ... ...

Schedule Impact

Signed Lead Engineer			Signed Comm. Manager	
Implementation	Approved	Not Approved	Change	Transfer to Inshore / offshore
Sign (Completions Manager)			Date:	
Change Closed Out Sign: (Commissioning Planning)			Date:	
NB: All signatures to be preceded by signatory initials (capitals)				

Illustration 28. Schedule Change Request form

45

Commissioning Schedule Change Request Register

No.	Description	Raised by	Sub System	Issue date	Planned return date	Actual return date	Issued to engineering	Issued to field (Comm.)
0010	Re-Allocate Activities	O. Berge	67.02-04	25.03.2014	25.03.2014	25.03.2014	25.03.2014	25.03.2014
0011	Delete Activities as listed	O. Hesj	69.05, 10,50	25.03.2014	25.03.2014	25.03.2014	25.03.2014	25.03.2014
0012	Re-Allocate Activities	A. Tuft	79.01 & 02	25.03.2014	25.03.2014	25.03.2014	25.03.2014	25.03.2014
0013	Extend Durations	O. Folke	70.05	25.03.2014	25.03.2014	25.03.2014	25.03.2014	25.03.2014
0014	Extend Durations	O. Folke	70.06	25.03.2014	25.03.2014	25.03.2014	25.03.2014	25.03.2014
0015	Extend Durations	O. Folke	70.07	14.04.2014	14.04.2014	14.04.2014	14.04.2014	14.04.2014
0016	Activity Required Earlier	T. Seter	70.11	14.04.2014	14.04.2014	14.04.2014	14.04.2014	14.04.2014
0017	Activity Required Earlier	T. Seter	70.12	14.04.2014	14.04.2014	14.04.2014	14.04.2014	14.04.2014
0018	Additional Scope Vendor	B. Holger	97.01					
0019	Additional Vendor Required	E. Aak	41.01,2,3	05.03.2014	05.03.2014	05.03.2014	05.03.2014	05.03.2014
0020	Ventilation Telecomm Equip.	E. Aak	90 Series	05.03.2014	05.03.2014	05.03.2014	05.03.2014	05.03.2014
0021	Temporary Fire Main	M. Munthe	00.30	05.03.2014	05.03.2014	05.03.2014	05.03.2014	05.03.2014
0022	Vendor Assist 600v Sw. Brd	M. Munthe	82 series	17.06.2014	17.06.2014	17.06.2014	17.06.2014	17.06.2014
0023	Additional Scope Vendor	B. Smith	92.01	17.06.2014	17.06.2014	17.06.2014	17.06.2014	17.06.2014
0024	Punchout Raise List	V. Gerde	96.04	17.06.2014	17.06.2014	17.06.2014	17.06.2014	17.06.2014
0025	Emer. Voice Transformers	J. F. Einer	91.02	17.06.2014	17.06.2014	17.06.2014	17.06.2014	17.06.2014
0026	Split Activity 80.06	K. Sorby	80.06	17.06.2014	17.06.2014	17.06.2014	17.06.2014	17.06.2014
0027	Turret Grounding	B. Smith	88.06	28.06.2014	28.06.2014	28.06.2014	28.06.2014	28.06.2014
0028	Replace Saturatable Reactors	C.M. cleod	97.01	28.06.2014	28.06.2014	28.06.2014	28.06.2014	28.06.2014
0029	DCC Punchout Activity	G. Young	All	28.06.2014	28.06.2014	28.06.2014	28.06.2014	28.06.2014
0030	Testing IGG Fan Motor	B. Smith	64.02	28.06.2014	28.06.2014	28.06.2014	28.06.2014	28.06.2014
0031								

Illustration 29. Schedule Change Request register

The "S" Curve

As a Manager you need to know where you are with respect to the plans you have laid out, where you have slipped or where you have made the most progress. If you compare progress to the original plan, you will know whether or not your project is staying on track. You need the facility to pin point your problems early. A good set of custom made reports produced each time you progress the network is essential to give you time to make the revisions and avoid extending the schedule end date.

The agreed progress 'S' curve gives you some leeway when reporting progress if you follow these points:

- Always run reports you are transmitting to the 'field' by early start.
- Confirm with your leads if they can achieve the goals being set
- Check that they are working on the right activities and if not, why?

The lead engineers would have had their input into the plan. There is no excuse not working on the agreed critical activities.

Your suite of reports should as a minimum include the following:

1. Bar charts that include the progress line. (Time now)
2. Which activities have slipped?
3. What is the status of the Critical activities?
4. Are there activities moving into the range of critical activities (labor or material related)? Look at the next 3 weeks or 3 months
5. Will the major milestone dates be affected?
6. What are the project costs?
7. How the workforce is performing and are their sufficient resources?
8. Has the finish date been impacted?

Use these reports in every status/progress meeting to make sure everyone understands that the plan has to be followed, or to align everyone around necessary agreed changes.

Commissioning Engineers, even though they have made all their inputs to the plan, tend to regard the plan as the "Planner's Plan," and not theirs. You have to break down that attitude and make the engineers, especially the Leads, fully accountable for their **activities as the plan laid them out.**

On the next page is a typical Early and Late start envelope

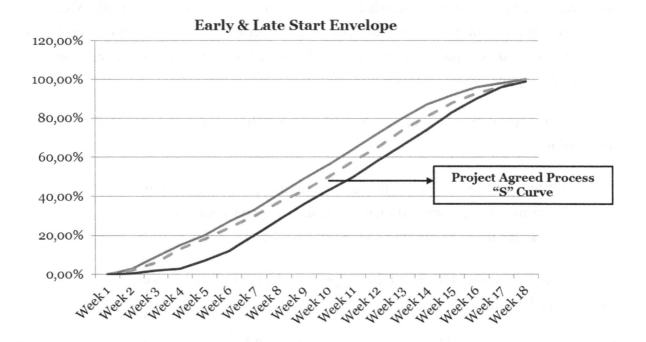

Illustration 30. Typical Early and Late start envelope

The Area-to-System Completion Transition

At a certain point in time you need to make sure that construction work is shifted from area-based to system-based. Obviously you will have to give Construction time to erect the steel, install all lighting, pull the majority of cables, install all the big equipment, etc. before the switch to system-based construction is done. It is not efficient to start system based construction until all the major equipment and vendor packages have been installed.

However, from that point in time it is hugely beneficial to start the "switch" and align the construction schedule with the Commissioning schedule.

The general experience is that it takes approximately 3 months to complete the switch, so the transition should start at least 2 months before module sail-away. In that way you will benefit from the system switch at the module yard, and more importantly, you will have all carry over work defined by systems, such that when the integration period starts, the Hook-up contractor is ready to start his program based on systems. Generally it will take the integration contractor at least 1 month to swing production to systems completion.

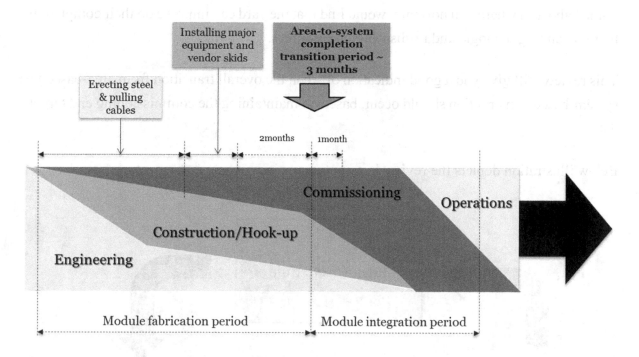

Illustration 31. Area-to-System completion transition graph

Review construction schedule

As the Commissioning Manager, you need to make sure that the construction program at the module yards does not jeopardize the overall commissioning schedule with its end target date.

You will need to check this at an early stage, say halfway through module completion, and review the construction program by linking it to the commissioning schedule to determine if you have a gap.

These are the simple steps you need to follow:

1. Review the construction schedule and look for general improvement areas.
2. Link the commissioning network to the module yard construction network and identify gaps
3. Identify overruns on commissioning target completion date

4. Cut the overrun by changing/improving the yard's completion logic, to suit system completion.

5. Make sure you aggressively follow up on the actions

Point 4 above is where you normally would find that the yard can improve on their completion by re-arranging the logic and re-distributing resources.

This review will give you a good indication of when the overall transition from area-based to system-based construction should occur, based on maintaining the commissioning end target date.

Below illustration depicts the review in a continuous improvement perspective

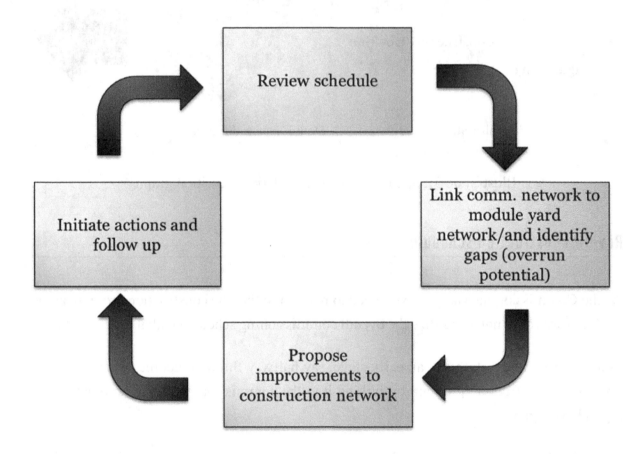

Illustration 32. Typical review circle

Estimating; Strategy, Tools and Considerations

Estimating Strategy

KISS – Keep it Simple Stupid

The following pages describe the recommended process from Hand Over from Construction through to Commissioning and how this process is broken down to make up the estimates. The "check and procedure" format is shown to help illustrate what needs to be included in the estimates, and empirical figures on % breakdown are also provided so that you can check if the estimates performed on your project are in the right "ballpark".

Traditionally, norms are given in man-hours per ton (per discipline). Man-hours per ton for commissioning is a very inaccurate way of presenting estimates as the systems you will have to commission bears no relationships to weight.

Although various attempts have been made to introduce so called "complexity indices", it never really captures the true scope of the job.

Therefore, we present figures in this chapter that we believe have never been published before, namely man-hours per system. That should bring you real close on your estimates!

Estimating is a "science" in its own right, and Project Control people like to play around with the numbers, "till their hearts content' as if estimating is a job in itself, and building the installation is something we do if we have time to spare.

If you want the job done, you apply the KISS (Keep It Simple Stupid) principle here as well.

Use experience figures both on the breakdown of each major element of the estimates as well as for the estimating of the individual activities. We obviously cannot provide estimates for the individual activities that can be applied industry-wide, as all projects are different, but based on numerous projects we do provide some interesting figures that give you a good feel for whether your estimates are in the correct order of magnitude. These figures are based on systems and are the general figures you should be looking at when adding up the individual activities that make up the estimate for the complete system.

One other important thing to remember when estimating is:

If prototype equipment or systems that have no proven operational history are being utilized, then a contingency factor needs to be added to the estimate, as inexperience with new types of systems and devices have an impact on the commissioning and Take Over schedule.

Estimate Elements Breakdown

When the construction department is ready to offer up a part system or sub system for "hand-over" to commissioning, the following should be implemented:

1. Commissioning team completes multi discipline pre-checks as detailed in section 2 below. On completion of the checks and review of the findings, a decision will be taken to accept or return the part system to construction for re-work. This hand-over will also include any punch points that construction has not completed.
   This pre-checking of the system generally comes under the visage of PRE-COMMISSIONING. It is estimated that this will take 10% of the allocated commissioning scope and duration.

2. The pre-check booklets are discipline orientated and developed to cover all aspects of the companies required standards, specifications and general layout of the equipment. All the pre-checks will be cleared against a pre-printed tag or major equipment list, with the sheet being signed off at the completion of the checks. A default agenda should operate and only parts that do not meet the requirements will be fully printed out on a separate sheet. By adopting this exception method, a huge saving on the amount of paperwork generated will be achieved. For example, work lists instead of separate sheets. If at any stage during the checks major recurring problems are encountered, then the checks will be stopped and the part system handed back to construction. It is strongly recommended that you develop such simple and cheap booklets for your project to avoid the bureaucratic and "no-value added" routines of endless sheets to cover the scope of the pre-checks.

3. Acceptance of the part system from construction then allows the start of proper commissioning, with completion of alignment checks, flushing checks, power checks, instrument checks, utility supplies or temporary supplies checked and all commissioning test records complete. It is estimated that this will take 25 % of the allocated commissioning scope and duration.

4. On completion of all the prerequisite checks, the part system can be filled or energized and ready for the dynamic commissioning to begin using the commissioning procedure

as a step-by-step guide. It is estimated that this will take the remaining 65 % of the allocated commissioning scope and duration.

Estimate Inclusions and Breakdown. Overall

The illustration below shows the elements that make up the total commissioning estimates and the percentage breakdown of these.

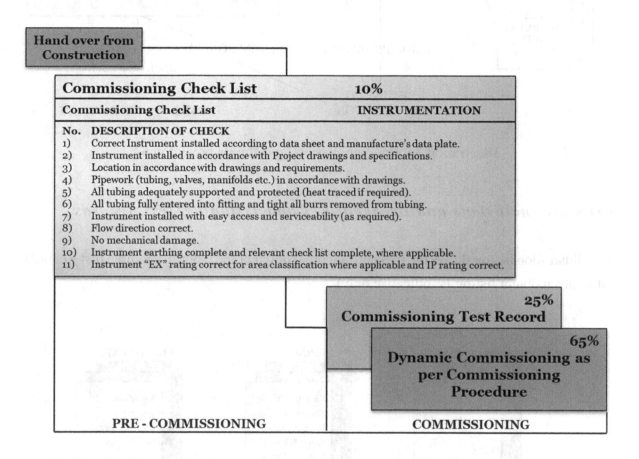

Illustration 33. Overall estimate breakdown

Estimate Inclusions and Breakdown. Pre-commissioning

The illustration below shows the elements that make up the pre-commissioning estimates.

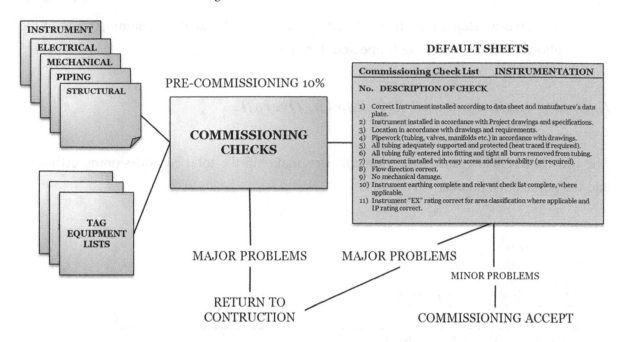

Illustration 34. Pre-commissioning estimate breakdown

Estimate Inclusions and Breakdown. Commissioning Test Records

The illustration below shows the makeup and breakdown of the Commissioning Test Records estimates (content listing is indicative only)

Commissioning Test Records 25%

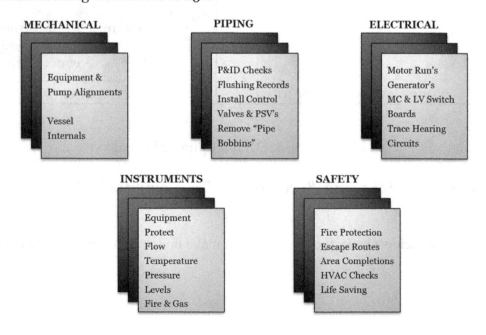

Illustration 35. Commissioning test records estimate breakdown

Estimate Inclusions and Breakdown. Dynamic Commissioning Procedures

The illustration below shows the makeup and break down of the Dynamic Commissioning Procedures estimates.

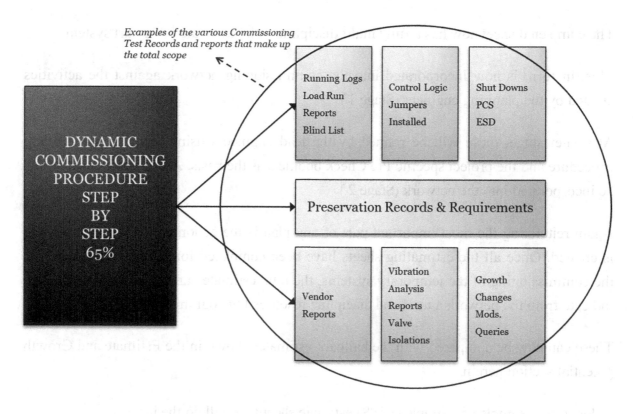

Illustration 36. Dynamic Commissioning Procedures estimate breakdown

Estimate Sheets

The following pages describe the process of the estimating sheet using the part system boundary drawings, the associated Tag listing numbers, PRE-Check Booklets and the Commissioning Procedures.

Again, back to the all-important boundary drawings. These will indicate the size of the part system; not too large to manage and not too small for Operations to take over. Using these, the planning engineer and commissioning manager will input the durations on to the estimate sheet including all the necessary labor splits and the required vendors for the dynamic part.

From this initial part, the planning engineer will input the required duration for the pre-commissioning multi discipline parts. Using the commissioning manual containing all the Commissioning Test records (CTR's) and depending on the complexity of the part system, the planning engineer will incorporate the durations. Also included would be estimates and duration's for the included Pre-Checks based on previous experience.

The completed sheet now has a fully multi discipline estimate related to a part system.

This, in turn, is now incorporated into the commissioning network against the activities created by the planning engineer (Stage 1.)

At a later stage, these will be refined by the lead engineers using their Commissioning Procedure and the project specific Pre Check booklets as the basis. Any changes would then be incorporated into the network (Stage 2.)

Again reiterating the most important part of any plan is the action you take after the plan is created. Once all the estimating sheets have been completed for all activities including the commissioning of the temporary systems, the total estimate can be seen. This will also indicate from the network a total and discipline resourced histogram.

These can now be compared with the ballpark estimates shown in the Estimate and Growth potential section herein.

Below is an example of a simple (KISS) estimate sheet that will do the job

Estimate Sheets

Commissioning Procedure NO. :			Area																				
System Description																							
Part System No. :			Description																				
Activety No.	Activety Description		Days																			Man-hours Required	
			1	2	3	4	5	6	7	8	9	10	11	12	13	14	15	16	17	18	19	20	
	PIPING / PROCESS																						
	PRE - Commissioning																						
	CTR's 6 Dynamic Commissioning																						
	MECHANICAL																						
	PRE - Commissioning																						
	CTR's 6 Dynamic Commissioning																						
	ELECTRICAL																						
	PRE - Commissioning																						
	CTR's 6 Dynamic Commissioning																						
	INSTRUMENT																						
	PRE - Commissioning																						
	CTR's 6 Dynamic Commissioning																						
	TELECOMM																						
	PRE - Commissioning																						
	CTR's 6 Dynamic Commissioning																						
	VENDOR																						
	Dynamic Comissioning																						
	OTHER																						
	PRE - Commissioning																						
	CTR's 6 Dynamic Commissioning																						
	Commissioning Assigned																						
Prepared by :			Date													Total Man-hours							

Illustration 37. Estimate sheet

Estimating Stage 1

Below is an illustration showing the concept of stage 1 estimating.

Estimating, stage 1

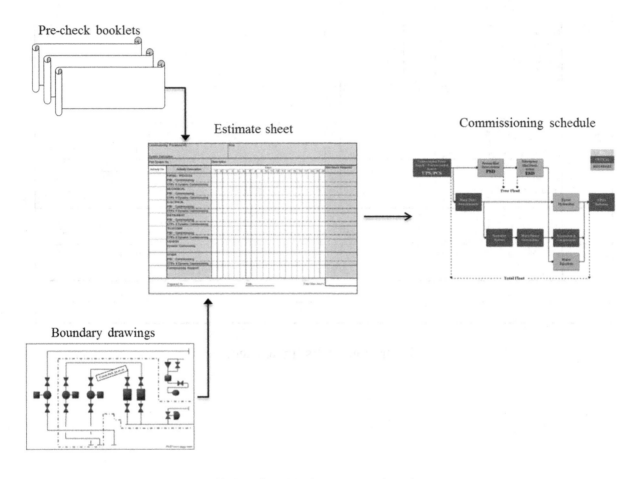

Illustration 38. Stage 1, estimating

Estimating Stage 2

Below is an illustration showing the concept of stage 2 estimating.

Estimating, stage 2

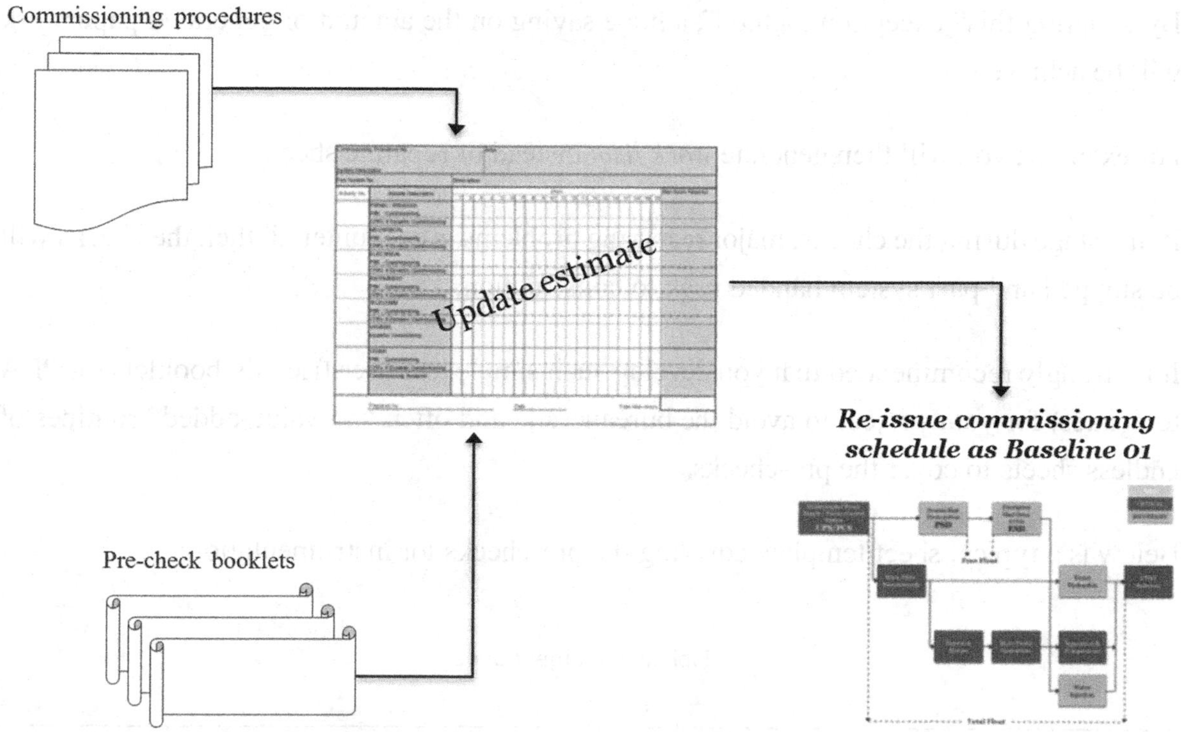

Illustration 39. Stage 2, estimating

The Check Sheets and Procedures

The pre-check booklet

These booklets are practical tools that will fit into the chest pocket of any coverall. Some companies have started to use pocket EX-rated PDA/tablets for check sheets and all other field checks that need to be documented, hence you have an even more practical on-line tool that directly links to, and updates the central database (PCS) as you complete your work in the field.

The pre-check booklets (or PDA/ tablet) are discipline oriented and developed to cover all aspects of the company's required standards, specifications and lay-out of equipment.

All pre-checks will be cleared against a pre-printed tag or major equipment list, and the sheet being signed off at the completion of the checks. A default agenda should operate, and only parts that do not meet the requirements will be printed/documented on a separate "sheet.

By adopting this" exception method", a huge saving on the amount of generated paperwork will be achieved.

For example; you will then generate *work lists* instead of separate sheets.

If any stage during the checks, major recurring problems is encountered, then the checks will be stopped and part system handed back to construction.

It is strongly recommended that you develop such simple and user-friendly booklets (or PDA templates) for your project to avoid the bureaucratic and often "no-value-added" routines of endless sheets to cover the pre-checks.

Below is a typical sheet/template covering the pre-checks for instrumentation

Typical Instrument Sheet

Commissioning Check List	Instrumentation
Instrument	Form No. I-CL-01

No	Description of check
1	Correct Instrument installed according to data sheet and manufacture's data plate
2	Instrument installed in accordance with Project drawings and specifications
3	Location in accordance with drawings and requirements
4	Pipework (tubing, valves, manifolds etc.) in accordance with drawings
5	All tubing adequately supported and protected (Heat traced if required)
6	All tubing fully entered into fitting and tight. All burrs removed from tubing
7	Instrument supported properly and adequately mechanical protected
8	Instrument installed with easy access and serviceability (as required)
9	Flow direction correct
10	No mechanical damage
11	Instrument earthing complete and relevant check list complete, where applicable
12	Instrument "EX" rating correct for area classification where applicable and IP rating correct

Illustration 40. Typical Commissioning pre-check template

The Commissioning Test Records

To assist in the completion of the Commissioning Test Records, each certificate has been compiled to give the technicians a defined scope of work. This applies to all disciplines across the project.

Below is an illustration of the typical Commissioning Test Record

The Commissioning Test Record

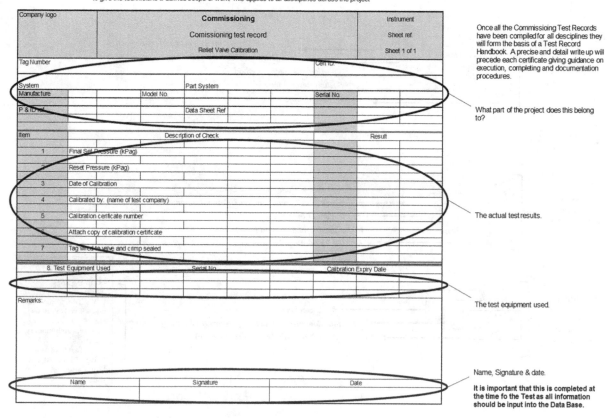

Illustration 41. Typical Commissioning Test Record

Commissioning Procedures

The Commissioning Procedure describes the actual step by step method of commissioning of the relevant commissioning package (part system). The completed and signed off Commissioning Procedure verifies that the work has been completed (the Audit Trail)

Procedures can be broken down in different ways, but make sure you have covered at least the elements shown in the below illustration.

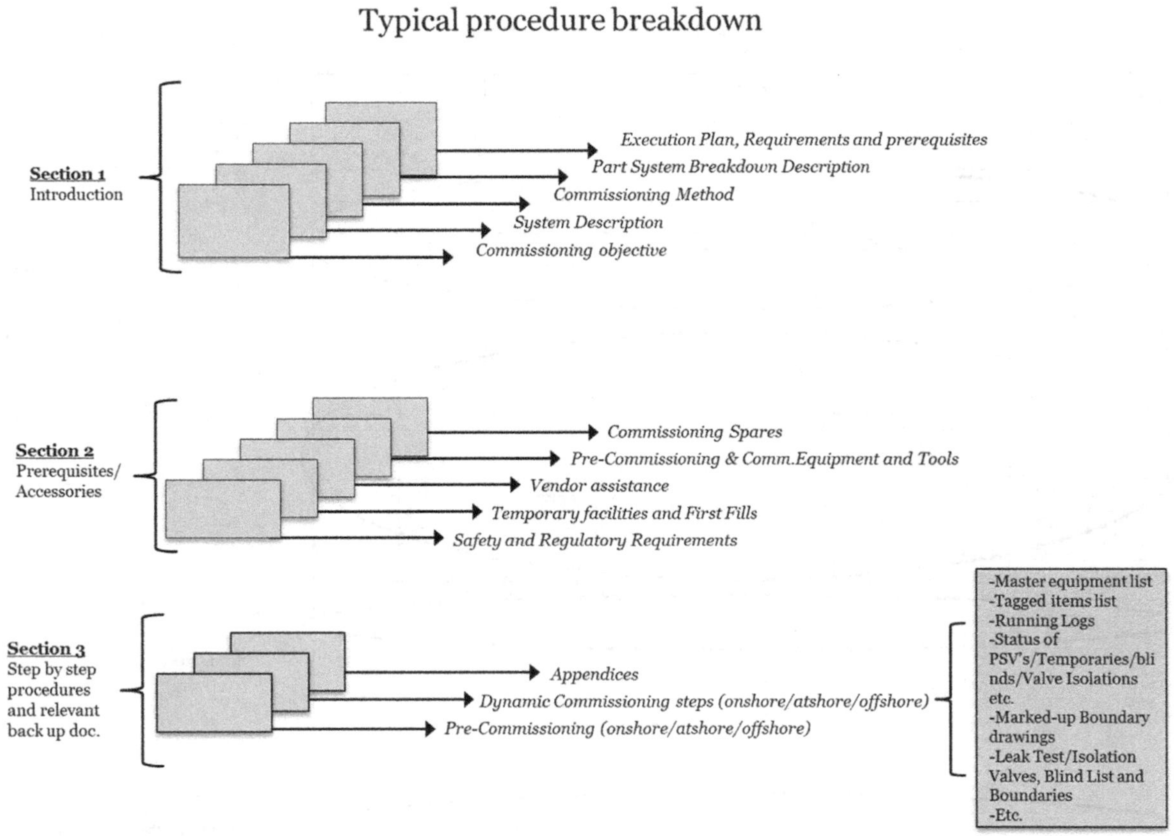

Typical procedure breakdown

Illustration 42. Typical Commissioning Procedure content

Commissioning Procedures as a Reporting Tool

In the same fashion as the "job card' or "task sheet" is the construction engineers' tool for identifying work, materials and reporting progress, the Commissioning Procedure is the tool used by the commissioning engineers to function test the equipment/systems and report progress.

You should keep progress reporting based on the procedures as simple as possible -KISS!

Don't fall in the "control every single step trap". It might be tempting to think that you can weigh every single step in the procedure and thereby have a super-accurate reporting tool at your disposal. Some companies actually do this, but only once. They soon find out that they waste valuable time on weighing and reporting while trying to be super-accurate.

Time they could actually have spent working, without losing the necessary accuracy required for reporting purposes by implementing a much simpler system.

An experienced commissioning engineer knows what his current progress is, and by implementing the simple scheme of putting a weighed percentage against the *major section* of the procedures, as opposed to every single step, you now have a simple reporting tool that also gives the engineers some freedom for adjustments based on their assessment of the current status.

So, weigh the major sections of the procedure, not every step!

Estimating and Growth: Figures and Factors

Estimates and Growth Potential

Estimating is usually based on the scenario that all goes relatively smooth and that is the way it should be.

So we estimate the time it will take to do the job under "normal" circumstances and maybe add a little experience-based contingency. We don't plan for disasters!

As explained in this book, all does not always go well. If you have not dealt with, or prepared for the issues raised in this book, you can expect your estimates to grow significantly.

The following pages give you some very interesting and useful figures and factors that you can apply to your project to see if you are in the right "ballpark."

It is obviously very difficult to provide construction figures for the large variety of fixed platforms that exists. This is due to the fact that so many different concepts are being used, such as Gravity Base Structures (GBS), Steel Jackets, a combination of the two, Jack ups, Tension Leg platforms, etc. These all have different building schemes with module lift onshore, module lift and construction offshore, a combination of the two, etc. The gathering of construction data for these is an enormous task and would not significantly enhance the value of this Commissioning oriented book.

Construction figures and growth on FPSO's, especially those coming out of Asian yards are very consistent. That is consistently high! Some real life data is provided both on Construction and Commissioning to aid in your estimating and growth expectations (potential). 17 real life examples are given, and these match with most of the FPSO's where hulls have been built in Asia. However, commissioning figures are quite universal regardless of platform concept and are provided on the next pages. The figures are based on FPSO's, but can be universally applied across platform concepts.

Generally, regardless of platform concept (on large projects), the number of systems to commission is the same, around 90-105 systems (project coding manual numbers). The complexity of the systems varies, but on average the estimated hours to commission them are the same.

We have gathered data on commissioning estimates on numerous projects and provided you with an average system estimate figure that as far as we know has never been published before. This will be a very useful checkpoint for your estimate.

Apply this figure on large multi-module projects: ***1350 hours per system***.

Use this figure to check if your estimate is in the right "ballpark"!

However, *this is just the basic estimates*. Now you will have to start including all the other activities that we describe in this book so that you will arrive at an estimate that reflects reality and will not see much growth.

Estimating "Ball Park Figures" for FPSO's

Consider man-hours at the integrated construction yard. This section will enable you to check the quantity of commissioning and construction hours you have estimated on your project.

Apply the *5 check* points below

1) Take the number of systems you have defined on your project and multiply by 1350, as explained on the previous page.

2) Take a normal size commissioning team of 90 direct men working 60 hours per week multiplied by duration in weeks. Generally 24 weeks, approximately 6 months. Our experience on commissioning of FPSO's would normally coincide with these numbers.

3) Compare (Real Project estimate figures)

Project	No of systems	Average estimate hours per system figure (1350)
A	99	133.650
B	105	141.750
C	100	135.000
D	107	144.450
E	103	139.050
F	105	141.750
G	88	118.800
H	92	124.200
I	89	120.150
J	100	135.000
K	104	140.400
L	87	117.450
M	99	133.650
N	98	132.300
O	111	149.850
P	99	133.650
Q	103	139.050

(These numbers above compare to 90 men x 60 hours x 24 weeks = 129,600 hours)

Note: These 17 real life projects match most FPSO's we have checked where the hulls have been built in Asia. They also match most other types of large installations we have checked that have a module-to integration-yard project completion scheme.

Is your project within this range? Well, this is your first and basic checkpoint!

Growth, FPSO's

4) Unless you seriously deal with and resolve the major issues discussed in this book you can expect your estimates to grow when measured in actual hours. In addition there will always be unknowns that will drive the hours up.

The numbers in the table below show how the scope changed for the actual projects on the list in 3) above.

Project	Commissioning original estimate	Commissioning actual
A	133.650	326.106
B	141.750	345.870
C	135.000	329.400
D	144.450	352.458
E	139.050	339.282
F	141.750	345.870
G	118.800	380.780
H	124.200	366.900
I	120.150	360.760
J	135.000	410.825
K	140.400	450.654
L	117.450	432.008
M	133.650	501.200
N	132.300	545.860
O	149.850	422.322
P	133.650	433.088
Q	139.050	411.900

These numbers from real life projects tell us you can expect a growth factor of around 2, 44 from the original estimate.

This is the factor you will need to reduce as much as possible!

If we consider the CONSTRUCTION side of projects from an *estimating* point of view, experience numbers tell us that these numbers are **4, 98** greater than the commissioning numbers.

Applying the factors to the construction side of the project would with our real life examples look like the once in the table below. Basically this means that if Construction has estimated all their hours, the commissioning estimated hour should come in around 5 times less.

Project	Comm. estimate	Comm.-to Constr. experience factor	Construction estimate
A	133.650	4,98	665.577
B	141.750	4,98	705.915
C	135.000	4,98	672.300
D	144.450	4,98	719.361
E	139.050	4,98	692.469
F	141.750	4.98	705.915
G	118.800	4.98	591.624
H	124.200	4.98	618.516
I	120.150	4.98	598.347
J	135.000	4.98	672.300
K	140.400	4.98	699.192
L	117.450	4.98	584.901
M	133.650	4.98	665.577
N	132.300	4.98	658.854
O	149.850	4.98	746.253
P	133.650	4.98	655.577
Q	139.050	4.98	692.469

Applying the factors to FPSO's

5) Apply the following experience factors to your specific project and check the status of your estimates and where you could potentially end up.

You should try to estimate as accurately as you possibly can. The *actual* commissioning numbers we present in this book are made up of all the various elements described herein that have so often been forgotten to include, or risks (typically some of those from the generic risk tables later in this book) that are not accounted for in the various phases of the project..

Summary of experience factors to consider:

Number of systems per the coding manual x 1350 hours = Commissioning estimate

> *Commissioning estimate x 4,98 = Construction estimate*

> ***Commissioning estimate x 2,44 = Commissioning actual***

> *Construction estimate x 2,42 = Construction actual*

Below is the full table with experience factors applied to the projects we investigated.

The *project total column* number is what you should expect the total hours to be, provided the experience factors are correct.

Project	Commissioning estimate	Commissioning actual (expected)	Construction estimate	Construction actual (expected)	Project total (expected)
A	133.650 x 2,44	326.106	665.577 x2,42	1.610.696	1.936.802
B	141.750 x 2,44	345.870	705.915 x2,42	1.708.314	2.054.184
C	135.000 x 2,44	329.400	672.300 x2,42	1.626.966	1.956.366
D	144.450 x 2,44	352.458	719.361 x2,42	1.740.853	2.093.303
E	139.050 x 2,44	339.282	692.469 x2,42	1.675.775	2.105.057
F	141.750 x 2,44	345.870	705.915 x2,42	1.708.314	2.054.184
G	118.800 x 2,44	380.780	591.624 x2,42	1.710.900	2.091.681
H	124.200 x 2,44	366.900	618.516 x2,42	1.800.777	2.177.677
I	120.150 x 2,44	360.760	598.347 x2,42	1.902.510	2.263.270
J	135.000 x 2,44	410.825	672.300 x2,42	1.945.970	2.356.795
K	140.400 x 2,44	450.654	699.192 x2,42	2.001.090	2.451.744
L	117.450 x 2,44	432.008	584.901 x2,42	1.870.070	2.302.078
M	133.650 x 2,44	501.200	665.577 x2,42	1.970.980	2.472.180
N	132.300 x 2,44	545.860	658.854 x2,42	2.017.333	2.563.193
O	149.850 x 2,44	422.322	746.253 x2,42	2.100.400	2.522.722
P	133.650 x 2,44	433.088	655.577 x2,42	1.900.800	2.333.888
Q	139.050 x 2,44	411.900	692.469 x2,42	1.667.138	2.079.038

It is interesting to see how the experience factors from a total project perspective compare to actual completion numbers.

Below is the table showing how the total *actual numbers* came in compared to the theoretical *total* in the table above.

Project	Total project estimate	Total project actual
A	1.936.802	1.939.936
B	2.054.184	2.387.000
C	1.956.366	1.931.850
D	2.093.303	2.096.908
E	2.105.057	2.017.948
F	2.054.184	2.058.234
G	2.091.681	2.111.788
H	2.177.677	2.199.555
I	2.263.270	2.333.333
J	2.356.795	2.345.467
K	2.451.744	2.456.666
L	2.302.078	2.340.340
M	2.472.180	2.489.444
N	2.563.193	2.577.644
O	2.522.722	2.580.933
P	2.333.888	2.312.233
Q	2.079.038	2.890.566

As can be seen from the table above, the factors come in within 1-3% accuracy, except for Project B, where we do know that both the main firewater pumps had to be changed out very late in the completion phase.

For all practical purposes this means that the quoted experience factors are more than accurate enough to use as a benchmark figure for *all* multi module integration projects whether it is an FPSO or any other type of platform installation.

So to summarize: *The benchmark figures you should be checking your commissioning estimates against on your project are the number of systems from the coding manual multiplied by 1350 hours.*

The construction estimate would be approximately 5 times the commissioning estimate.

This should give you a very good starting point for your initial estimating job.

It is time to check it out on your project!

SUMMARY-Key Success Factors in the Planning Phase

✓ Define your key performance indicators (KPI) early and make sure they are meaningful, understandable, simple, easy and will work as a precise status follow up tool.

✓ Define your reports up front, and make them simple and user-friendly.

✓ Design a few simple back-up reports that allow you to track progress when the system is down.

✓ Develop the commissioning boundary drawings in the early engineering phase, utilizing senior commissioning personnel.

✓ Make sure the boundary drawings definition represents commissionable entities that can be handed over to Operations.

✓ Do not mix commissioning packages on the same drawing sheets, however; make reference to other packages, and connection points.

✓ Make sure all identified design changes required to accommodate a trouble-free commissioning are implemented.

✓ Make sure you define the hand-over philosophy in line with your definition of part systems. Avoid the "basic function" philosophy.

✓ Utilize a simple estimating strategy and check estimates against benchmark figures. Check for hour per system figures.

✓ Build all activities into the plan, including vendors, vendor assistance, commissioning and de-commissioning of temporaries, re-alignment work, paperwork activities, boroscoping etc. In this way you will avoid surprises later.

✓ Make sure you close-link the static and dynamic commissioning activities as much as possible

✓ Define and communicate the schedule's critical path early.

✓ Early development of commissioning schedule to prioritize construction work represented in a fully developed and integrated construction/commissioning schedule.

✓ Derive the vendor schedule directly from the commissioning schedule.

✓ Always run and distribute the schedule based on early starts.

✓ "Force" a system based construction in late module yard/early integration yard phase.

✓ Simplify reporting based on commissioning procedures (dynamic activities) by using sections, as opposed to single checkpoints.

2.0. PREPARATIONS

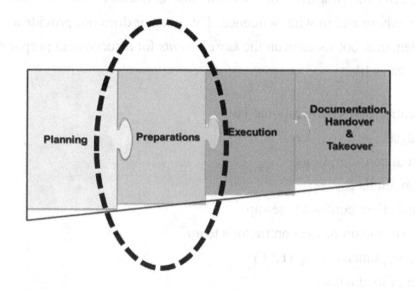

- Organization and the value chain
- Audit/Gap review
- Risk analysis
- Preparations specifics
- FPSO specific considerations
- Summary: Key Success Factors in the Preparation phase

Preparations

If you are not properly prepared, you will struggle to maintain control!

After you have had a small senior team in place to complete the work described in the previous chapter, you need to start thinking about what kind of organization you will need for the next phases of the project and how you want that organization to interact with all the other players on the project. You will also have to consider how you will prepare for all the practical issues that will ensure a streamlined execution of the activities described in your schedule.

This chapter discusses the organizational issues you need to consider, and other practical stuff to be worked on after the first draft of your schedule is released. You now know what you will commission, where and in what sequence. This chapter does not provide a complete list of preparation elements, but focuses on the *key elements* for a successful preparations phase. We will discuss issues like;

- Value creation and organizational issues
- Risk analysis
- Contractual considerations
- A view on alliances
- Traditional client/contractor set-up
- Auditing your team or the contractor's team
- Factory acceptance testing (FAT)
- Provision of load banks
- N2 testing of compressors onshore
- Subsea issues and FPSO specifics

Organization and the value chain

Value Creation from an organizational perspective

In the context of a Project Organization, creating value and preventing value loss, means making sure that all the players understand that they are part of a bigger picture with one ultimate goal. Time lost because of organizational interface issues, poor processes, organization or capabilities equal value loss, hence equal schedule threats and dissatisfaction from the end customer.

It is worthwhile for you, as a manager to spend time with the organization explaining the concept of Value Creation and the Value Chain, and frequently reviewing with your team the effectiveness of the organization and its processes to optimize value creation in all elements of the value chain.

This is known as achieving customer focus.

The illustration below depicts the key stages in adding value (value creation) and how it relates to your project.

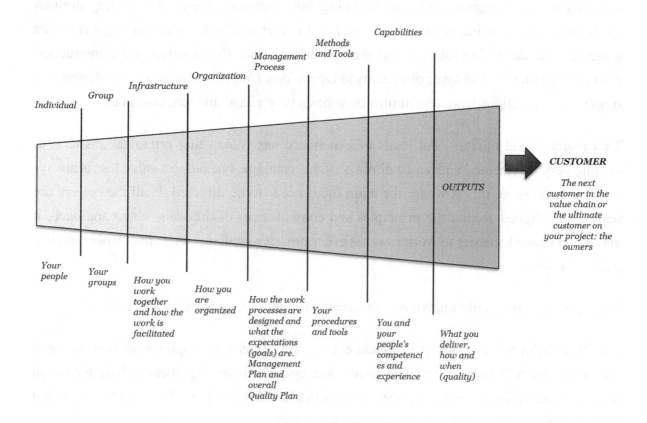

Illustration 43. Generic value creation chart

The Value Chain

The Value Chain is a healthy way to look at any business to understand the customer /supplier relationships. This would also apply to this industry and project completions. We are not talking about your traditional suppliers of equipment and services and how you relate to them, but how the various sections or departments of the Project internally relate to one another.

It is especially valuable to spend time with the various players, explaining and defining the customers / suppliers relationships and how these roles vary with the various stages of the project. In the early conceptual design stage, before contracts are awarded, the engineering department will see no real hard customers. As the project evolves, the construction department becomes their main customer.

If you, as the Commissioning Manager, hope to have any early influence on engineering, you need to make sure they understand that you are an important customer that sets requirements to design and other deliverables. As the project further evolves, the Construction department becomes the main supplier to Commissioning, but as design changes are coming through all the time, Engineering is still a key supplier. In other words, Commissioning has at this stage become the main customer and sets the priorities for Engineering and Construction work. Once you start handover of systems to Operations, Commissioning will be viewed as a supplier to Operations who now in turn becomes a very visual and real customer.

This might sound obvious, but loads of experience has shown that organizations tend to operate very fragmented and hence diminish value creation. The biggest value loss is always in the interfaces, so this is where the main focus needs to be directed. If all the players are seamlessly aligned around the principles and consequences of the value chain approach, it makes it a whole lot easier to work towards every project's goal: *deliver to the owners on time and on budget.*

This is what's commonly known as *"achieving customer focus in the organization".*

The illustration below shows the gradual change in the customer/supplier relationships and depicts the most important activities undertaken by commissioning in each phase for which they need deliveries from the suppliers. (Activities in brackets [] are delivered by others but form important input to the commissioning activities).

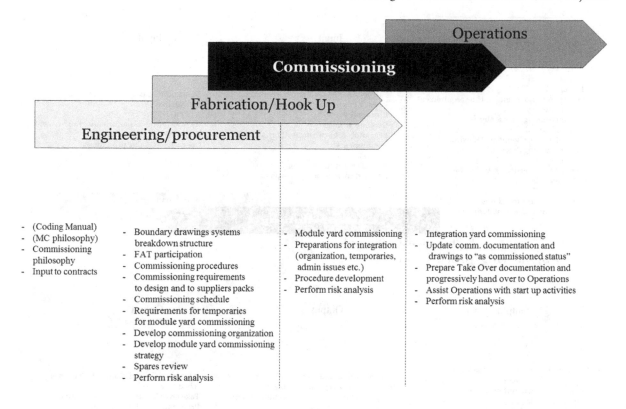

Illustration 44. Value chain gradual change graph

The Value Chain- Input/output chart

The Value Chain input/output chart below shows the various inputs and outputs related to each specific phase of the project. I.e. which inputs that will be required in order to produce specific outputs that are required at the various stages of the project.

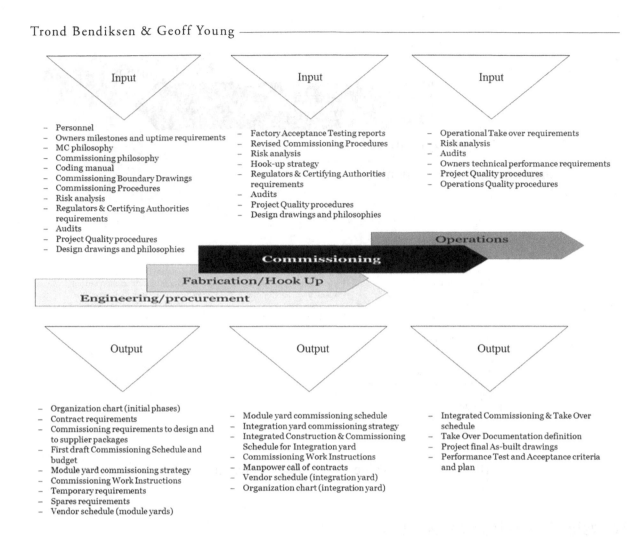

Input

- Personnel
- Owners milestones and uptime requirements
- MC philosophy
- Commissioning philosophy
- Coding manual
- Commissioning Boundary Drawings
- Commissioning Procedures
- Risk analysis
- Regulators & Certifying Authorities requirements
- Audits
- Project Quality procedures
- Design drawings and philosophies

Input

- Factory Acceptance Testing reports
- Revised Commissioning Procedures
- Risk analysis
- Hook-up strategy
- Regulators & Certifying Authorities requirements
- Audits
- Project Quality procedures
- Design drawings and philosophies

Input

- Operational Take over requirements
- Risk analysis
- Audits
- Owners technical performance requirements
- Project Quality procedures
- Operations Quality procedures

Operations

Commissioning

Fabrication/Hook Up

Engineering/procurement

Output

- Organization chart (initial phases)
- Contract requirements
- Commissioning requirements to design and to supplier packages
- First draft Commissioning Schedule and budget
- Module yard commissioning strategy
- Commissioning Work Instructions
- Temporary requirements
- Spares requirements
- Vendor schedule (module yards)

Output

- Module yard commissioning schedule
- Integration yard commissioning strategy
- Integrated Construction & Commissioning Schedule for Integration yard
- Commissioning Work Instructions
- Manpower call of contracts
- Vendor schedule (integration yard)
- Organization chart (integration yard)

Output

- Integrated Commissioning & Take Over schedule
- Take Over Documentation definition
- Project final As-built drawings
- Performance Test and Acceptance criteria and plan

Illustration 45. Value chain input/output chart

Process orientation of project completion

Sometimes you might be in a position to influence the whole project relative to organizational set up and management concept, and sometimes (most of the time) you are not.

If you happen to be in a position whereby you can influence the above, you should seriously be thinking about introducing a *process oriented completion system*, and organize all of the completion activities in line with a process view along the value chain of work.

Process orientation is a predominant trend in the Operations world, and are slowly gaining acceptance in the Project Development world as well. So far, however, very few companies have done a complete switch from a procedural to a process way of organizing their project development work, although some have started to take on this concept in the completion phase of projects.

It is however, a relatively manageable change that is required should one decide to instigate a switch to process orientation.

The conceptual execution model of process orientation is described below.

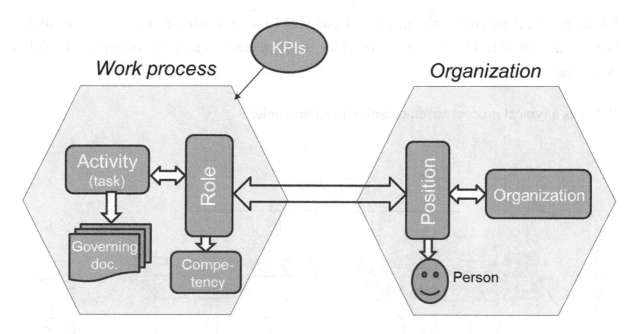

Illustration 46. Process orientation, conceptual execution model.

The conceptual model explains the relationships between the work process elements and the organizational elements. The model is centered on the all-important *"role"* element that connects to specific activity (tasks), where the activities are linked to the governing documentation required to perform a specific activity. Hence competency must be linked to the role in as much as the role performs activities that require competency.

In this way the whole execution model itself becomes independent of who does the work as long as the person that fills the role has the required competency to do so. This means that if you re-organize the project, it has no bearing on the execution model as the tasks remain the same (work has to be done regardless of what your organizational set up looks like). Someone will have to fill the roles, it is just a matter of who (which position or person) you link to the role.

Utilizing such a model makes it is clear that organizing your team in value chain process perspective will enhance the focus on execution and final delivery, and decrease focus on how the actual organizational chart is drawn.

Consequently you should establish a value chain organizational model that focuses primarily on driving the activities to completion through horizontal processes defined by the required activities and not by a "silo view" as to which organizational unit should perform them.

For all practical purposes this means that you will have to nominate *process owners* that become accountable for driving all activities to completion, regardless of organizational belonging.

Below is a typical process based organizational principle.

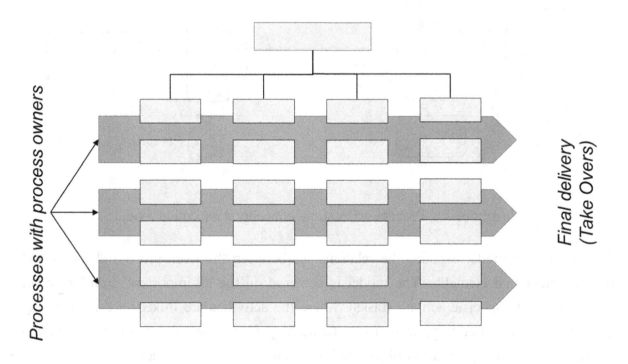

Illustration 47. Process based organizational principle

Process orientation has among others, the following advantages:

- Clear and easily understandable roles vs. responsibilities (as opposed to RACIs)
- Roles and associated activities govern how work is being performed, not organizational structure.
- Enhanced focus on execution and final delivery

- As workflows are visible across organizational boundaries via dedicated roles, interfaces are efficiently streamlined and seamless.
- Easily accessible information to activity governing elements (checklists etc.) for each activity.
- Easily accessible authority regulations information (directly linked to relevant activities)
- Easy progress reporting, directly in system (no paper) as well as real time visible progress status.
- Easy KPI follow up
- Vast reduction in paper documentation (70-80%)
- Compatible with field carried PDA/tablets and remote system access and input
- Easily managed nonconformance and change control
- Enhanced focus on final delivery (product)

If one decides to switch to process orientation, the following activities are required:

- Procure a process oriented management system.
- Describe all main commissioning processes in flow diagrams (swim lanes) instead of procedures.

  For example:

    - Commission main seawater pump
    - Commission main power generators
    - Commission HVAC system
    - Etc.

- Take all activities that normally would be a "procedural main element" (heading) for the various main processes and break them down into manageable activities (tasks). Include any regulatory requirements.
- Take all the details that normally would be a "procedural step" and link them to the correct activities in the flow diagram, including any activities to be executed or witnessed by regulators.
- Identify all roles responsible for the activities (tasks) in each swim lane (derived from procedures)

- Organize the "extended" Completion Team along the value creation process, i.e. include all contributors to final Take Over (e.g. include procurement, engineering and HSE in the same matrix like organization). See chapter *"Organizing for success"*
- Link the already identified the KPIs
- Define your Lead Engineers as process owners and accountable for performance of their specific processes.
- Upload all information above in the process oriented management system

Below is an example of a flowchart concept from a typical process oriented management system.

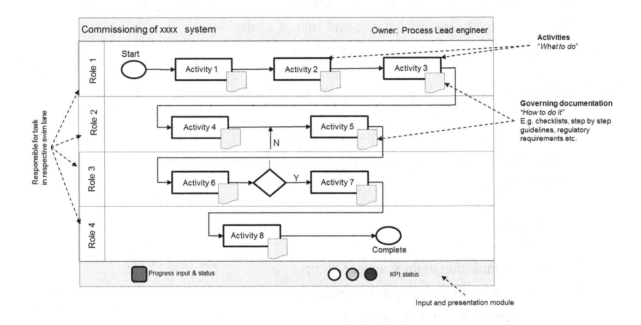

Illustration 48. Process flow chart concept

We see process orientation as a tremendous advantage as explained above, but as most companies still operate the "old fashioned" way, we have chosen to build this book mainly around that concept. However as explained above the switch is a relatively "small job" once the decision to go process oriented is taken, and even if you don't do a full switch we strongly recommend that you set up the completion organization in a process structure as explained under "Organization" below.

Organization

Your organization is the primary tool for an effective execution! Hence you should spend time ensuring that your organization is put together in a way that secures a streamlined execution process. Obviously competency assurance is a crucial prerequisite of any organization, which goes without saying, but all too often organizations are "haphazardly" put together without much of a holistic approach.

For all practical purposes this means that you should view the whole commissioning phase as the basis for how the organization is put together, taking into account the pre-module yard phase, the module yard commissioning, any transitional phases (for example sailing phase), the integration yard work as well as the offshore phase. By viewing the total picture you will be much better off in planning your resources and setting up a streamlined and interface-efficient organization.

The organization you'll need for the initial phase, say module yard completion, is obviously different from what you will need when all modules are ready to be integrated into one entity.

However, for continuity reasons, and for the benefit of the project, you need to consider the whole picture from the outset.

The easiest way to do this is to "start with the end", meaning you will first have to consider what kind of organization you need at peak load. Then, work your way back towards the early phase, and fill the initial positions based on these requirements, and then work your way to the future offshore phase and possible integration with Operations for the start- up period.

To maintain this concept, you will need to nominate a Commissioning Lead at each module yard reporting into a "home office ", and who will later assume a lead position at the integration site.

The idea is simply to make sure you utilize your "long term" lead personnel in the initial module phase to ensure continuity and knowledge transfer to integration yard and later offshore as the illustration below depicts.

The illustration below depicts the personnel flow principle.

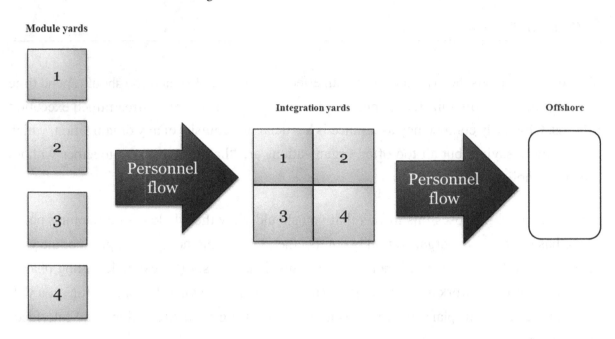

Illustration 49. Module to integration yard-to offshore personnel flow principle

Make sure you develop role descriptions that are clear and concise. A useful instrument to bring clarity to roles is to specify the various tasks and responsibilities in a RACI (Responsible/ Accountable/Consult/Inform) chart. A RACI chart specifies who is Responsible for the tasks (the "doer"), who is Accountable (where the bucks stop), who do you need to Consult (who has input) and who do you need to Inform (who needs to know).

If your project is supported by a *process oriented management system*, roles are clearly marked against all activities for each role, and the work instructions are linked to each activity. In that way you'll have a clear and concise relationship between roles and responsibilities, visualized in flow charts for all work processes. This is a much better system, easier to use, understand and maintain, than the "old fashioned" RACI model that requires a manually maintained spreadsheet model and does not provide the same clarity.

Although we definitely favor the process oriented management system, it is not the system you use/prefer that is the most important question. What's important is that you actually make sure you instigate absolute clarity on roles and responsibilities!

The "home office" concept will function as continuity assurance until all modules are installed at the integration yard.

The illustration below depicts the concept of "maintaining continuity", and still accommodate the requirements for early module yard commissioning.

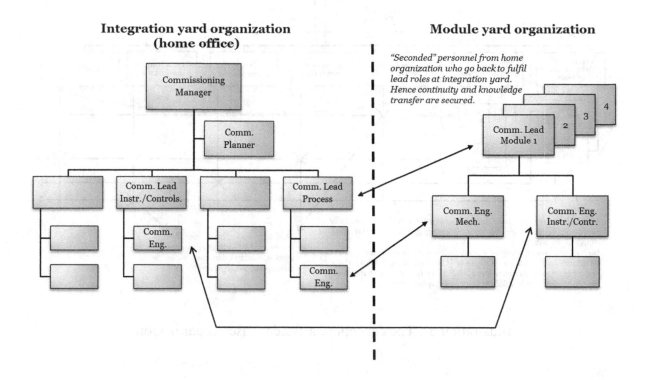

Illustration 50. "Home office" continuity concept

Another important aspect of your organizational structure is making sure that the organization reflects the concept of commissioning; namely completion by SYSTEMS.

You should build the structure around Systems Leads and recruit the necessary discipline engineers under this systems structure. The only two disciplines that warrant a discipline approach are Electrical and Instrument as these both are systems oriented in their own rights. These two disciplines also support all other systems leads, and hence will have to work in a matrix type approach.

As your commissioning gets started you want to make sure that your leads understand they are accountable for completing systems and part systems, not just disciplines.

The illustration below shows the concept of a system based commissioning organization.

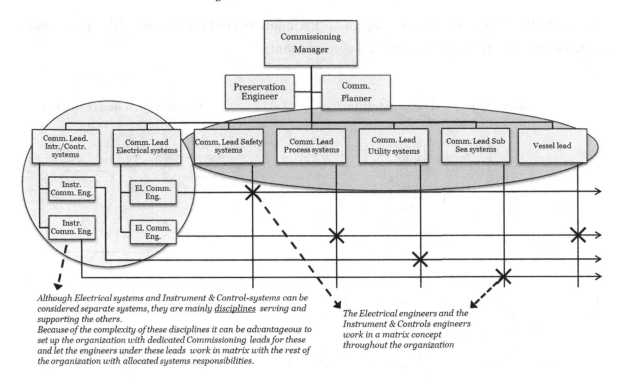

Although Electrical systems and Instrument & Control-systems can be considered separate systems, they are mainly <u>disciplines</u> serving and supporting the others.
Because of the complexity of these disciplines it can be advantageous to set up the organization with dedicated Commissioning leads for these and let the engineers under these leads work in matrix with the rest of the organization with allocated systems responsibilities.

The Electrical engineers and the Instrument & Controls engineers work in a matrix concept throughout the organization

Illustration 51. The concept of a system based organization

The Staffing Profile

One of the biggest failures when staffing the Commissioning organization is starting the recruitment process too late!

Although understanding the importance of having commissioning personnel recruited early is gradually maturing, a lot of project managers still think that commissioning is a last minute thing that ; "we'll fix when we get there".

It is extremely important for the streamlining of later phases of a project to recruit the right commissioning personnel *early* to make sure that the design accommodates Commissioning's needs;

- That all boundary drawings are developed and refined
- That the input to the all-important Factory Acceptance Testing purchase orders are done
- That the temporary equipment requirements for module yard commissioning are identified and ordered

- That the spares are identified and ordered
- That the Project Completion System is being populated correctly
- That the commissioning strategy is developed etc.

As a general rule you will eventually gain a lot more than you initially spend by recruiting the key commissioning personnel early rather than later in the project.

On the next page is a typical staffing profile for a multi-module project

Below is a typical staffing profile for a multi-module project

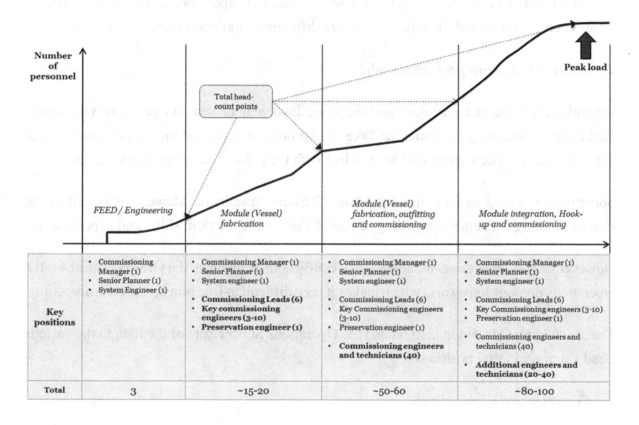

Illustration 52. Typical staffing profile for a multi module project

Other important elements of building a successful and responsible organization are:

1. Selection of personnel.

The project's success will depend on the quality of the personnel that you have recruited! This is where you need to be really careful. To put it bluntly, recruit people you know, and in turn recruit people these persons know.

Do not rely on or be impressed by CV's alone. 25 years of experience can easily be 1 year of experience 25 times, and there is a significant difference; don't you think?

2. Involve Operations personnel early!

Operations are the end customer and the more involvement you can get from Operations during commissioning, the easier the Take Over process will go, and the greater commitment you will receive. These guys will have to live with the product for years down the road.

Sometimes it would be ideal that the future Offshore Installation Manager is put on as the Commissioning Manager, (providing of course that he has the right skills and experience).

However, at this level there are always task conflicts in as much as the OIM is crucial for the Operations preparations work, which makes it very difficult to free him up for commissioning.

The second most ideal step is to second the Operations Supervisors or the like, to the various Lead Commissioning positions

3. Customer and supplier view.

Don't blend the Construction and Commissioning organization into one unit. Some major industry players have a very ideal view of project completion, such as believing that the ideal organizational concept is to combine Construction and Commissioning in one soup of an organization. This does not work! Why? You cannot be both customer and supplier at the same time. (Reference is made to the previous Value Chain Discussion.)

Construction and Commissioning, although they should seamlessly come together, have very different focus areas, and organizationally mixing the two only leads to one or both losing focus on their main objectives.

As we have explained earlier the driver for the construction work is the Commissioning Schedule.

To ensure that the construction work is planned in line with this, hence ensuring a streamlined and trouble free interface, Commissioning needs to be in the "driving seat" from the outset. It is truly surprising that with all the projects that have struggled with this important interface, still companies maintain the old fashioned model of mixing Construction and Commissioning in one group.

The "standard" approach has been to recruit a so-called "Hook Up and Commissioning Manager" who will run both Hook Up and Commissioning. Obviously the early Construction phase will get the focus, just to find out down the line that the commissioning requirements where forgotten and suffer the often significant consequences.

When are we going to learn? How many more spectacular failures will it take before we understand that it will pay dividends to organize the projects with a Commissioning Manager who in the very early phase of the project devises the plan with the right priorities, and requests Construction to be complete in that order?

Hence, we will make the case that the Construction Manager should report to the Commissioning Manager. Maybe not initially, but at least after all the major bulk material and heavy equipment/ skids are installed.

This would then be aligned with the universally recognized customer/supplier principle, and the organization should reflect this.

4. *Organizational barriers.*

Break down organizational barriers and focus the whole organization on the end result, the Takeovers. Build a "task force" structure to enhance accountabilities across the board!

Once commissioning is well under way at the integration site and construction work starts to ramp down, it is advantageous to initiate a task force meeting structure that incorporates all the various players, suppliers and customers in the value chain, to enhance accountabilities across the whole project organization.

The meetings should focus solely on the end Key Performance Indicator from commissioning, namely the progressive takeover of systems by Operations. All the players at the table are responsible for their respective issues that can hold up the Takeovers, such as, Materials, Design Queries, Operations & Maintenance manuals and Regulatory issues etc.

Focus hard on, and constantly visualize the Take Over progress and issues holding you up. In this way the team members will soon understand the important role they play in making sure that the Take Overs do happen according to the plan.

The "tasks force" structure is shown below.

The illustration below is an example only and does not necessarily include all members of a task force concept.

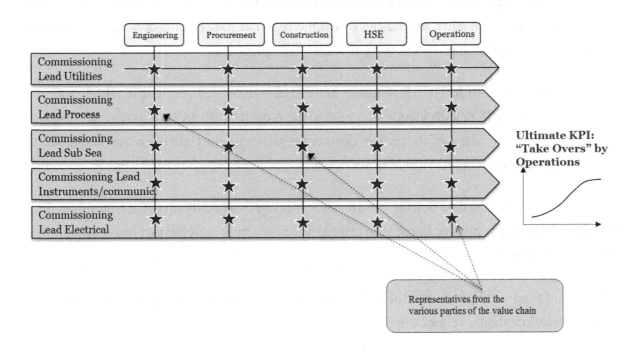

Illustration 53. Typical task force, process oriented organizational structure

Organizing this way will effectively represent a shift from Job descriptions to Team Accountability. In usual bureaucratic project organizations, individual roles are specified in terms of "job descriptions" which enumerate each individual's duties and responsibilities.

In extreme cases, members of staff will not carry out certain tasks if they do not fall within the list of duties for which they are responsible.

Instead of individual job descriptions, groups of individuals are held accountable for what they do, their "output'. Goals, in this case, the overall KPI –and the planned Take Overs by Operations, are set in broad terms through role models and accountability is reflected in the progress measurement systems.

By adopting a team based accountability structure, the old axiom of management, "what gets measured, gets done" is a lot easier to maintain and live by both for you as the manager and for the individual team members.

This concept, however, will not work unless you as the manager understand that in a team structure, empowerment is the key to success. If you have succeeded in visualizing the measurable goals of the project to the team members, and get positive feedback, that without doubt confirms everyone has understood the goals, you are then in a position to give the necessary freedom required for the team to deliver "the goods" by empowering the team members.

The word, empower means to enable and give authority. Work groups are enabled when they have the necessary skills, tools and techniques. They have authority when they can make the necessary changes or decisions without seeking approval.

Your job, as a manager for an empowered team, is to make sure they have all the necessary tools and skills at the table to make the right decisions, measure the performance based on the agreed KPI's and take actions on variations.

Your task as Manager is not to control every little detail of the job, that's your team's responsibility.

Organizing Assistance Manpower

Often Hook-up and Commissioning share the trades labor pool during project execution.

This has one big disadvantage that tends to impact the schedule, namely the rivalry between Hook-up and Commissioning in terms of scrambling for resources.

If this interface is not working perfectly, with processes in place to control it, it can be detrimental to the schedule. It is very difficult in a hectic project environment not to fight for resources, as each part of the organization looks after their own scope.

To maximize efficiency from the work force, this element should be built into the labor agreement for the sites, in such a fashion that commissioning have their own dedicated labor pool which they control 100% of the time.

In unionized environments, this is particularly important in order to avoid unnecessary and time-consuming demarcation issues.

In these environments, you will have enough internal demarcation issues between various trades *within* Commissioning, so you do not want to deal with Hook-up / Commissioning demarcation issues as well.

Contractual Considerations and Implications

There are different methods of contractually organizing commissioning responsibilities on a project. In pursue of the most cost effective contractual concept, some companies have left all commissioning to the fabricators and in some recent cases to the integration contractor.

On a multi module project, it does not take much imagination to see that such a concept is disastrous. Even the thought of leaving the commissioning to the fabrication contractor on a single module job is scary enough.

Why?

A fabrication or hook-up contractor's core competency is just that: to fabricate and hook-up, nothing else. Of course most of these contractors recognize their limitations in this respect, so they team up with a company or persons that have the right competencies, thinking they have got it made. Sadly, history tells us that the contractor attempts to build an alliance with an engineering company thinking that, because they are designers of systems, they must also be able to commission the systems as well, fail in all cases.

Commissioning is a very specialized type of work that requires a very specific skill set, normally only retained within operating companies and special commissioning companies. In periods with lack of recruitment and downsizing in the industry, even the operating companies do not have a lot of people in-house with this skill set. To then trust that a fabrication / hook-up contractor can do the job is lack of sound management judgment at best, and gross negligence at worst.

If there is no way around it, because the management team has decided that this is the way it shall be, there are two things you absolutely must do in the very early stage of the game:

1. Put a detailed audit-or gap analysis program in place.
2. Make sure you "infiltrate" the contractor's organization to a maximum extent with competent commissioning people

The latter you will have to negotiate with the contractor, but the audit-or gap analysis you are free to carry out as a client activity when and as required. (See auditing in this chapter).

Alliances

If you find yourself working on a project that is set up as an alliance, where all the alliance partners are contractually responsible for their own engineering and deliverables, you will most likely be struggling.

It is our informed opinion and bitter experience with alliances that they simply do not work well enough. Worldwide official benchmarking studies support this view. That is also the reason why most big operating companies now steer clear of alliances and move back to the more traditional model, although enhanced with what is recognized as "preferred contractors and suppliers-concept".

However, it is usually not your decision how the overall project is organized. You are only hired to make sure everything works and that the owners get what they have paid for.

So again, if you are working inside an alliance as the Commissioning Manager, you will most likely have to deal with issues such as, taking onboard commissioning personnel from the various alliance partners that you don't really want or need, working with different specifications for the various alliance partners, deliveries, overcoming huge interface issues, going through endless discussions with the partners about engineering deliverables, design freeze timing, software development and interfaces with other suppliers, etc.

Effectively, you will become the project's main interface coordinator.

The most important thing you will have to do early is to make sure there is a maximum degree of consistency in terms of the commissioning processes. Make sure you do this by performing an alliance wide audit, or gap analysis on commissioning using the elements specified in the next chapter. Basically, perform an audit as you would audit your own organization or any contractor's organization. Make sure you infiltrate the various alliance partners' organizations as much as possible.

The only recognized advantage with an alliance model is the concept of making it easy to ensure all partners are aligned and focused on the end goal due to financial incentives. It's called the "gain and pain share" concept. It has however, proved to be extremely difficult to make this concept work efficiently on relatively short-term oil and gas projects. No wonder it in many quarters are sarcastically termed "the blame share concept".

The illustration below, "alliances- the spider web challenge" looks very busy and confusing. That's the whole point. The illustration is only meant to drive home the very point that *it is* a confusing and difficult concept!

The illustration below shows an example of a true alliance concept. Each alliance partner is fully responsible for his own work and the delivery of a fully "integrated" functioning unit.

Note: The below is a real life example. Concepts and challenges may vary depending on alliance set-up and contact philosophy.

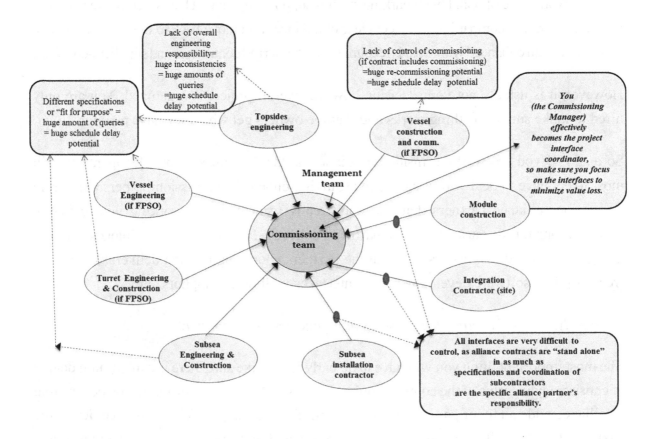

Illustration 54. Alliances- the Spider Web challenge

Traditional Contracts

Traditional client/contractor relationships are sometimes referred to as "hard money contracts". This is not wholly true. The term "hard money contracts" should only be used in the context of fixed price contracts with only pain-share elements built in. If gain-share elements are built into a fixed price contract, it is not a "hard money contract". If you have built in reimbursable elements, or the whole contract is reimbursable, then it is obviously also not a "hard money contract". "Hard money contracts" has not a lot of advantages seen from a commissioning point of view. If the contract includes commissioning, you are into the scenario discussed earlier about contractor's lack of commissioning expertise, a very difficult change environment and a big potential for re-work, resulting in schedule delay.

On a more traditional client/contractor relationship, with a "preferred contractor scheme", normally meaning that incentives in terms of pain and gain-share are built in, your chances of success viewed from a commissioning standpoint are much greater. Traditional contracts, for the time being are the preferred way and give you more leeway in terms of influencing the way commissioning is being planned and executed, simply because the traditional financial elements allow for it.

You are more likely to have clearer responsibilities defined, simpler interfaces, more "hard control" over the contractor, easier access to sub-contractors and less discussions when changes are required (as opposed to in an alliance).

There are obviously various advantages and disadvantages with both alliances and traditional contracts, but from a commissioning viewpoint, a traditional contract is the preferred option.

Auditing/Gap review

The intention of this section of the book is not to devise a complete audit concept like approach, team staffing, reporting and follow up, because there are plenty of books out there covering auditing as a subject. It is simply the intention to outline the typical process and in particular the questions that you will need to ask when performing an audit-or gap review on commissioning.

Keep It Simple Stupid -KISS !

The questions in such an audit/gap review are very standard, self-evident, and do not vary much from project to project.

The trick is, however, to structure these questions so that by the end of the audit/gap review you can see, "the total picture"

You should structure the questions in sections as shown in the example on the next pages.

This should give you an easy and organized way to deal with the actions you put in place to close the gaps.

The next pages are examples of how the audit/gap review can be organized.

The illustration below depicts the audit/gap process in a Continuous Improvement perspective

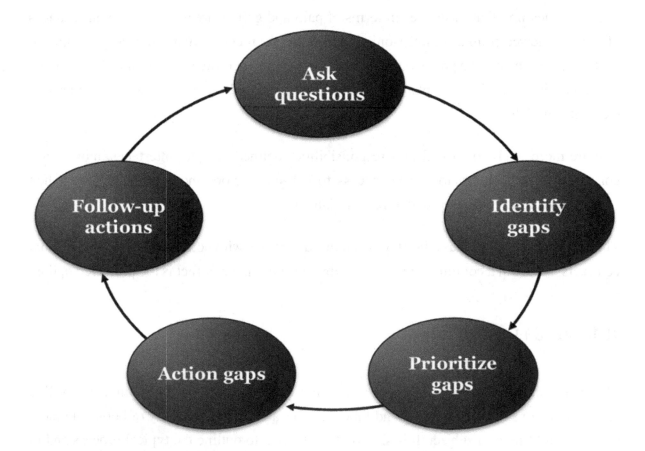

Illustration 55. The Audit/Gap review in a Continuous Improvement perspective

Auditing the contractor, or self - auditing your team (Gap review)

In auditing or gap review of the construction/commissioning contractor, or auditing own organization, you need to make sure that all the details are covered. Such an audit/gap program should at least include the elements shown in the table below.

Note: What you audit/review will obviously vary with the project phase (timing), so the elements covered in the below table may not be relevant for all phases.

No	Element	Checks / Comments Are the following in place/ being adhered to

1	*Procedures and manuals- General.* Check what general procedures and manuals exist to support the project execution phase	• Commissioning Manual
		• Project Commissioning Philosophy
		• Commissioning strategy
		• Mechanical Completion Manual
		• Planning philosophy/procedure
		• Punch List procedure
		• Progress reporting structure
		• Commissioning (Design) Query system
		• Permit To Work system
		• Livening Up Notice
		• Electrical isolation
		• Mechanical isolation
		• Commissioning Jumper/by-pass log system
		• Blinding list log
		• Hand Over to Operations procedure
		• Software Change control system/procedure
		• Vendor coordination procedure
		• Preservation philosophy/procedure
		• Certifying authority requirements
		   ✓ witness points
		   ✓ hold points
		   ✓ specific requirements

2	*Organization.* *Check to ensure that the organizational set- up is right?*	• Is the organization chart fully developed?
		• Do job descriptions /role descriptions exist?
		• Is the manpower right for the job?
		• Is the discipline make up right?
		• Is number of Operations personnel in the Comm. Team sufficient?
		• Is the group make up right?
		• Is the responsibility split/lines of responsibilities clear?
		• Are the interfaces with MC/Construction Engineering and interfaces with Operations clearly defined?
		• Are interfaces with other project teams clearly defined?
		• Is the assistance manpower pool available and are call off routines in place?
		• In a union environment, are trade demarcations clearly identified and understood by everyone?
		• Has a structured commissioning meeting schedule been established?
3	*Planning.* *Check to ensure that all aspects of planning and reporting to support project execution are in place and that all the right personnel has given input to the plan.*	• Are detailed plans in place for the various stages?
		• How is/has input to the plan been processed?
		• Who has checked/verified the plan?
		• How have priorities been established?
		• Have commissioning identified work priorities?
		• How has the planning logic been formatted and who has given the input?
		• Who has established durations?
		• What has been used to establish duration's- standard test sheets?
		• Are hours included for dynamic commissioning?
		• Are Vendor execution hours included?
		• Are Vendor assistance hours included?
		• Are assistance execution hours to Operations included?
		• Are hours included for re-commissioning activities?
		• Are hours included for re-alignment work?
		• Are hours included for document handover preparations?
		• Are hours included for document handover preparations?
		• Are hours included for commissioning/ de-commissioning of temporaries?
		• What is the method of reporting?
		• How are the reports to be presented?
		• Are routines in place for schedule change control?

4	*Commissioning Procedures.* *Check to ensure that all the procedures are identified/developed, and that they are suitable for the job to cover off all requirements in a quality fashion.*	• Are procedures are available covering all commissioning activities? • Is there a commissioning procedure index? • Is there a commissioning procedure completion plan with clear responsibilities identified? • How is progress on the procedure completion plan reported? • Is there a project approved revision control system in place? • Is the procedure lay out including space for sign off upon completion and/or for regulatory witness sign off? • Do they include P&ID's commissioning boundary limit mark-ups? • Who has reviewed the procedures and how is it controlled? • Do the procedures include a prerequisite list? • Do the procedures include a safety section? • How was the various discipline input covered by responsible engineer? • Where is the controlled master copy kept?

| 5 | *Commissioning budget.*

Check to ensure that all requirements are covered to support an efficient execution. | • Check budget provisions for the following and ensure sufficient funds allocated or covered by separate contracts:
　✓ Man-hours including;
　　o supervisors, engineers, technicians
　　o vendors, vendor assistance trades
　　o commissioning assistance
　✓ temporaries
　✓ spare parts
　✓ consumables
　✓ lubes
　✓ first fills
　✓ test equipment
　✓ radios
• Utilities including water/diesel/power
• Nitrogen leak testing
• Load bank(s)
• Hydraulic flushing |
| 6 | *Commissioning system.*
Check databases, allocations etc. to ensure consistency, user friendliness and traceability. | • Check P&ID and Single Line Diagram, Comm. Boundary drawing mark ups
　✓ Are all packs identified
　✓ Are all packs uniquely numbered
　✓ Are boundary splits at natural break-points
• Status of Commissioning Check Sheets allocation
• Check status of linking of MC packs to Comm. Packs
• Check fields of Commissioning Database
• Check prerequisites list for completeness |

7	*MC system.* *Check MC databases and system to ensure consistency, user friendliness and traceability.*	• Check status of MC test sheet allocation in the MC database • Check MC pack allocation per system/part system to ensure all equipment is covered • Check MC reporting procedures, update frequencies etc. • Has Commissioning checked and confirmed MC test sheet allocation. • Confirm how vendor pack equipment has been covered for MC completion • Confirm how punch lists from FAT's are being covered and cleared • Check that Hand-Overs to commissioning are planned on a system/part-system basis and that the MC completion sheets reflect this • Check that regulatory issues -PL's are covered in the MC database
8	*Preservation.* *Check to ensure that an adequate preservation system is in place and that resources have been nominated.*	• Who is responsible for preservation during commissioning? • Is there an overall preservation program in place for all phases of the project? • Who maintains the composite list of preservation requirements for preservation program/vendor packages system and resources? • How is other equipment than vendor packages covered? • Do records exist for the preservation of equipment/packages since leaving vendor works? • Is preservation deficiency recorded in the Commissioning/MC databases? • How are preservation records going to be handed over to Operations?

9	*Factory Acceptance Testing (FAT).* *Check FAT records, participation etc. to ensure quality data and information.*	• Does Commissioning have a copy of the FAT's conducted by the project? • Who participated in the FAT's (did Commissioning participate)? • Do any punch lists exist as part of the FAT - documentation (MC and Commissioning)? • List any packages that was not part of FAT's • List any packages that completed FAT but were not witnessed by an engineering or commissioning representative.

10	*Vendors.* *Check system for vendor management to ensure an efficient support during the various stages of the project*	• Does Commissioning have a full list off all vendors required for commissioning?
		 • Has an estimate been completed on the durations required for vendor commissioning activities for all phase of the project (onshore, at- shore, inshore, offshore)?
		 • Have contracts been arranged with vendors for commissioning assistance?
		 • Has an estimate been completed for the vendor assistance budget and what was the basis for the estimate?
		 • How does Commissioning plan to track vendor hours and is there a method of allocating hours to work activities other than commissioning e.g.:
		    ✓ engineering work/updates
		    ✓ clearing of punch lists
		    ✓ hours used clearing vendors own problems/ faults
		    ✓ stand-by time
		 • For the relevant packages, has a rotation for vendors been established?

| 11 | *Safety.* *Check "safety system" to ensure a safe execution of Commissioning.* | • Does a safety procedure exist and does it identify areas of responsibility?
• Is a Permit to Work system in place and ready to implement?
• Is a Livening Up procedure in place
• Does a procedure exist covering electrical and mechanical isolations?
• Has the Construction work force been instructed on the workings of the Permit to Work system?
• Is it clear who the responsible parties for all types of permits are?
• How is Construction advised of Commissioning activities?
• Do the Commissioning procedures cover a safety section relevant to the commissioning activities that are due to take place?
• Does the Contractor have a safety plan/procedure in place for the fabrication phase?
• Are the Commissioning Group fully aware of the procedures?
• Is there a nominated commissioning representative to liaise with the contractor safety personnel?
• Has the Commissioning Group attended a site safety induction course?
• Is there a schedule for regular safety meetings?
• Who keeps the minutes from the safety meetings? |

| 12 | *Hand-Over to Operations.* *Check Hand-Over system to ensure a streamlined and efficient process* | • How are hand-over of systems handled between Commissioning and Operations?
• Who is the nominated representative(s) for Operations?
• Has Operations been involved in any of the commissioning activities?
• On what basis are the Hand-Overs accepted by Operations?
• Does a Hand-Over certificate exist?
• Is there a procedure that describes the Hand-Over process and all relevant documentation to be complete upon Hand-Over, covering such as;
   ✓ punch lists
   ✓ material required to complete the work
   ✓ marked up boundary drawings
   ✓ as-build status
   ✓ jumper lists
   ✓ blindings registers
   ✓ safety check lists
   ✓ vendor reports
   ✓ signed commissioning Procedures
   ✓ commissioning Check lists
   ✓ outstanding Queries list
   ✓ preservation records
   ✓ vendor reports, etc. |

13	**Test equipment.** *Check that test equipment is identified and that adequate controls of this equipment are in place.*	• How has the test equipment requirements been established? • Have the commissioning engineers been involved or reviewed the requirements? • Does a composite list exist for all test equipment? • Is it proposed to hire or purchase the equipment? • Does any list differentiate between vendor test equipment that is supplied as part of a vendor call out procedure? • How is relief valve testing being covered • How is pressure cylinder re-fill covered • How is the calibration of the equipment recorded? Is there a composite list identifying the calibration validity? • How and where is the test equipment stored? Who has control on issuing the equipment? • Does the list include commissioning radios? If not, how are these covered? • Is Commissioning involved in the startup of the equipment for permanent use?
14	**1st Fills/Lubes.** *Check to ensure that all first fill requirements are covered.*	• Who has the responsibility for the first fill? • Does a composite list exist covering all first fills and lubricants? • How has the budget been established and is it sufficient? • Are all contracts for supply of first fills and lubricants in place? • How and where are first fills and lubricants to be stored?

15	**Utilities.** *Check to ensure that all required utilities such as water and diesel are adequately covered.*	• Has a list been generated covering all utility support for commissioning? • How have the estimates been established? • Do separate contracts exist for the supply of utilities such as diesel, water, steam etc.? • How and where are they to be stored? • How has the budget been established and is it sufficient?
16	**Temporaries** *Check to ensure that all required temporaries are Covered.*	• How have the temporary requirements been established for commissioning? • Who has the responsibility for supplying and installing? • If Commissioning is responsible, how are the contracts for the major items to be covered? • How and who has established the duration's for the equipment? • Who is responsible for the running and maintenance of the equipment?
17	**Spares.** *Check to ensure that all spares and spares management is adequate.*	• Does a composite list covering all the commissioning spares required to cover the commissioning activities exist? • If a list exists, who completed the exercise? • Have the commissioning engineers reviewed the list? • Who is responsible for purchasing the spares? • Are the spares to be purchased through the project nominated supplier of the equipment? • Who is responsible for the top up orders? • Where are the spares to be stored? • Who is responsible for the issue of spares and how is it controlled? • How has the budget been established and is it sufficient? • Is there an agreement with Operations regarding use of Operations' spares if required?

18	*Commissioning assistance manpower.* *Check to ensure that adequate arrangements exist for the supply and usage of assistance manpower.*	• Who will Commissioning use as assistance for trades such as scaffolding, rigging, electricians, millwrights etc.? • How have the numbers been established for assistance? • Who had established the budget and what is it based on? • How are the numbers to be controlled on a daily basis? • Who is responsible for controlling the personnel and logging manpower – supply hours against each of the activities? • Does a schedule of rates exist for each type of trade and how much assistance manpower notice is required for the assistance? • Does Commissioning have complete control of the labor when it is allocated? • If in a union environment, have demarcation lines been clearly identified and understood by all?
19	*Regulatory/certifying bodies.* *Check to ensure that all regulatory and certifying authorities' requirements are covered and those relationships are managed in an effective way.*	• Has a regulatory/certification issues database been established? • Who is responsible for maintaining the database? • If the database is linked to the PCS database, If not, how is closure of items controlled? • Have all procedures been supplied to the regulating bodies/ certifying for their identification of witness points etc.? • Is there a nominated project person responsible for formal liaison with the regulating/certifying bodies? • How is the daily interface with certifying bodies handled?

Audit/Gap Review Follow-up

Once you have identified, prioritized and actioned the various findings, you need to make sure that you have a thorough follow-up system in place.

Again: apply the KISS principle!

The only thing you need is a simple spreadsheet with action, actionee, deadline and close out date registered on it. However, the spreadsheet alone does nothing for you. It is your persistent follow-up that will drive closure of the items. Use your weekly meetings for follow-up. Make it clear that you will not accept delays unless these are accompanied by some really good excuses. If deadlines are not met, and the excuses are valid, you should set new aggressive deadlines and follow-up in the next meeting.

If action deadlines fall between meetings, ensure that you follow-up directly with the actionee on actual dates.

It always helps to remind the actionees in advance that you will be asking for status on such and such dates!

Remember the old management saying:

Actions that are not aggressively followed-up will not be done.

Risk Analysis

Risk analysis is basically twofold.

First there is the high level management schedule risk analysis, where big ticket items such as module transport/module lifting, marine operations, sail-away considerations etc. are being assessed for high level schedule risks, and the P10/P50/P90 scenarios are developed.

The other part of risk analysis is the very important, practical analysis of "what can go wrong" and how to mitigate these risks. From a Commissioning manager's viewpoint, this is where you need to direct your team's energy.

Performing regular practical risk analysis or what we call Practical Risk Sessions (PRS), during commissioning is a prudent and effective management tool to identify issues that can be a threat to the schedule. These risk analysis are usually performed well into the execution phase.

What is not so usual however, but can be highly effective is to perform a thorough practical risk analysis exercise very early, before module integration, when you've had some experience back from the module yards, and to continue performing these at various stages of the game.

We will be discussing some typical risks based on experience, but before we do that it is useful to look at Risk Analysis in a Continuous Improvement perspective, as this process is a repetitive continuous Quality process. It is also useful to view two different charts that show the typical Engineering/Commissioning Queries distribution and the timing of these.

Below is an illustration that views risk analysis in a Continuous Improvement perspective and explains a practical methodology.

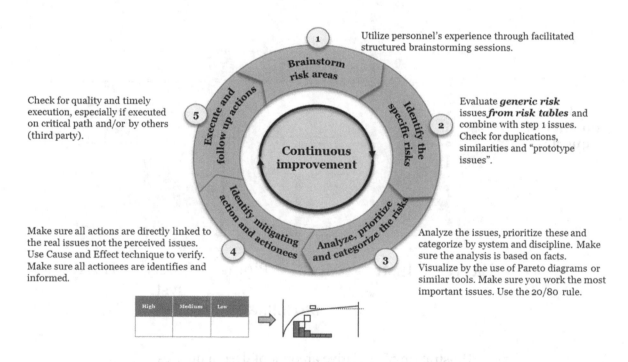

Illustration 56. Risk analysis methodology in a practical CI perspective

This Continuous Improvement Risk Process should be undertaken *at least* 4 times in a major project's life:

1) Halfway through the module completion phase

2) Just prior to the module integration phase
3) Halfway through the module integration phase
4) Just prior to the offshore phase

Design Queries

Design queries obviously represent a significant growth potential = risk potential on any project. I.e. you need to prepare for these risks!

The diagram below is a compilation of data from major offshore development projects from around the world, and how these relatively stack up.

Only the most "commissioning related" disciplines are shown.

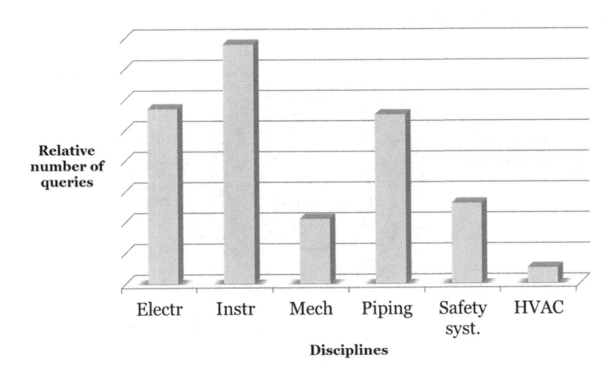

Illustration 57. Relative amount of design queries

The graph below shows the relative amount of Queries as a function of time (project phase) and indicates where the risk analysis should take place.

Note the two "up-front" Practical Risk Sessions (PRS).

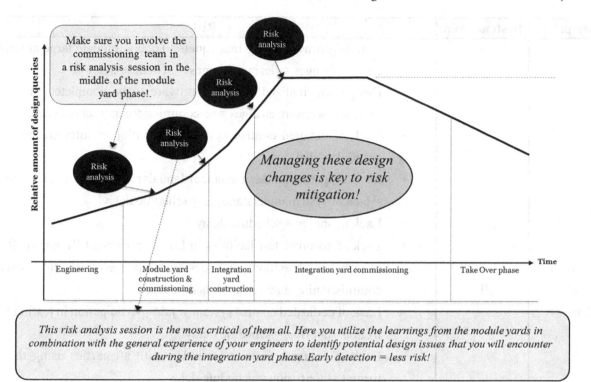

Illustration 58. Relative amount of design queries as a function of project phase.

Generic Risk Table

The previous charts tell us two things:

1) The disciplines from which we can expect the most issues (read design changes) = RISKS
2) When in the life of the project the issues will hit us the most.

The tables on the next pages are lists of generic issues = RISKS, and should bring you straight to the point in terms of some important areas where you should be looking for risks on your project

Note:

It is obviously not possible to list all issues you may encounter on a project. The issues on the list below are some of the important generic issues that you might come across, and does not in any way provide a complete listing of all possible risks. We have tried to stay away from too many pure design issues, and concentrated on the completion (construction/commissioning) related issues.

I.E. you've got a designed unit, and you work with what you have. However it is obviously impossible not to touch on any design issues in such a listing, so some of the unavoidable ones in relation to the specific risk issues are listed on the following pages.

Discipline	System/Area	Risk
Instruments & Controls	All	• Data Highway capacity inadequate to accommodate large amounts of design changes = design changes = schedule delay • Design not finalized to allow software to be completed thus saving extensive software changes = re-commissioning = schedule delay • Lack of detailed control system description = software changes = schedule delay • Lack of Operating & Maintenance Manuals prior to start of commissioning = lack of system understanding = schedule delay • Lack of spares = schedule delay • Lack of adequate test facilities in Local Instrument Rooms (LIR) such as portable OS station, data sockets, telephone outlets etc = extended commissioning duration's = schedule delay. • Lack of dedicated control system vendor participation in testing = slow trouble shooting = schedule delay • Lack of common instrument index with all parties using the same format = confusion = schedule delay. • Inadequate commissioning follow up of software testing at vendor works= changes at site = schedule delay • Lack of operations personnel involved with commissioning = lack of experience and system understanding = commissioning continuously being brought in to show Operations how system work = reduced efficiency and productivity = affecting schedule
Electrical	All	• Inadequate amount of heat tracing. Typically on low point drains and freeze exposed equipment. = equipment damage/design changes = schedule delay • Heat tracing designed by circuit and not by system = schedule delay • Inadequate electrical load available for load testing = not fully tested system, unknown performance = potential design changes= schedule delay (use load bank!) • Lack of spares = schedule delay • Inadequate preservation of equipment packages, and especially electrical heaters = repairs = schedule delay • Lack of operations personnel involved with commissioning = lack of experience and system understanding = commissioning continuously being brought in to show Operations how system work = reduced efficiency and productivity = affecting schedule

Mechanical	Utility and Process Systems	• Re-alignment of pumps/motors after module lift and draft changes= extended commissioning duration=schedule delay • Seizing of equipment due to inadequate preservation = equipment damage = schedule delay • Inadequate spares on major equipment packages/critical equipment = schedule delay • Lack of operations personnel involved with commissioning = lack of experience and system understanding = commissioning continuously being brought in to show Operations how system work = reduced efficiency and productivity = affecting schedule
Piping/ Process	Gas compression and Oil separation	• Lack of full N2/He test-run of compressors onshore (in countries where flaring is very restricted) = costly offshore troubleshooting = schedule delay • Lack of clear and uniform bolt tensioning and torqueing procedure = rework = schedule delay • Lack of standardization on gaskets = confusion = rework = schedule delay • Lack of understanding by construction for the importance of having minimum stress on compressor nozzles = rework = schedule delay • Poor high pressure ring joints installation (lack of training for construction pipefitters and foremen) = rework = schedule delay • Inadequate cleanliness of piping systems= equipment damage/ extended commissioning duration= schedule delay (boroscope all critical areas! And/or make sure commissioning thoroughly follow up on construction's pipe flushing activities. • Stroking of valves in contaminated piping systems= equipment damage= schedule delay • Inadequate spare seal kits for valves= extended commissioning duration = schedule delay • Not removing process isolation valves (or not remove balls) before cleaning pipework = valve damage = schedule delay • Lack of spares (in particular lack of pressure ring joints) = schedule delay • Lack of operations personnel involved with commissioning = lack of experience and system understanding = commissioning continuously being brought in to show Operations how system work = reduced efficiency and productivity = affecting schedule

Piping/ Process	Hydraulics	• Inadequate cleanliness/additional flushing = extended commissioning duration = schedule delay • Return line sizing to small/valve timing not adequate= design change= schedule delay • Lack of realistic flushing estimates. Unless a "super", hands-on person has done the estimate, double it! = schedule delay • Lack of operations personnel involved with commissioning = lack of experience and system understanding = commissioning continuously being brought in to show Operations how system work = reduced efficiency and productivity = affecting schedule • Lack of spares = schedule delay
Safety Systems	Firewater/ Deluge All Areas	• Lack of coverage = design changes = schedule delay • Inadequate preservation of valves in dry systems = equipment damage(dried out seals) = schedule delay • Deluge testing: a) Deluge discharge testing is a major disruptive commissioning activity that affects both construction and commissioning b) is a regulatory requirement that such tests are conducted and therefore any mitigation measures that can be taken in order to minimize the risk of having to re-perform or extend such tests should taken c) One such measure is to perform a joint engineering, construction and commissioning punch out prior to pressure testing and installation of the nozzles. The second is to ensure that all piping systems are thoroughly flushed. d) To leave either of these activities until deluge discharge testing can and will result in nozzles having to be relocated, nozzles being blocked by foreign matters etc., the consequence of which is re-testing=schedule delay. • Lack of spares = schedule delay • Contamination due to inadequate temporaries = system/equipment damage = schedule delay: Generally the permanent firewater pumps are not available or cannot be utilized for the initial phase of the commissioning of the firewater system and temporary units are usually employed. In selecting temporary firewater supplies, adequate provisions must be in place to prevent contamination of the permanent system • Lack of operations personnel involved with commissioning = lack of experience and system understanding commissioning continuously being brought in to show Operations how system work = reduced efficiency and productivity = affecting schedule

Safety Systems	Fire & Gas All Areas	• If prototype equipment or systems that have no proven operational history are being utilized, then the commissioning schedule for these systems should be carefully planned and contingencies added to duration's. • Inexperience with new types of systems and devices = impact on the commissioning schedule. • Lack of spares = schedule delay • Lack of consumables such as calibration gas etc = schedule delay • Lack of consistent master documentation: One master set of Fire & Gas Cause & Effect sheets must be maintained by the Lead F&G commissioning engineer. Commissioning engineer, regulatory bodies, certifying authorities etc., should use this master for witnessing signatures. Deficiencies of such = re-testing = schedule delay (especially if commissioning and witnessing is performed in shifts. • Since Fire & Gas detection devices and systems require regular maintenance, calibration etc, the Take Over by Operations of such systems should preferably be on an area basis. Take Over of the total F&G system after the completion of all commissioning activities will result in commissioning having to perform a continuous PM program on the operational system = expending the commissioning scope and increasing risk of the systems being rejected at Take Over = schedule delay • Lack of adequate amount of CCR screens available for commissioning of F&G. (The quantity required is function of the commissioning schedule, the number of fire areas and the number of F&G commissioning personnel). = schedule delay • Lack of operations personnel involved with commissioning = lack of experience and system understanding = commissioning continuously being brought in to show Operations how system work = reduced efficiency and productivity = affecting schedule • Inadequate PA coverage = design changes = schedule delay
Safety systems	Gaseous Extinguishing systems	• Recharge facilities must be available locally. Pressurized cylinders cannot be air-freighted and an accidental discharge = delays and possible impact on one of the major commissioning milestones, e.g. Start-up of the main power generators. Alternatively spare cylinders must be available.

Safety systems	Portable Fire Extinguishers & Miscellaneous safety equipment	• Failure to have the required certification at Take Over = schedule delay. • Portable fire extinguishers are delivered certified. However, extinguishers require re-certification on an annual basis. It is unlikely that Take Over of this equipment would be within the initial 12 months certification, and re-certification would therefore be required prior to Take Over. Failure to have this certification in place at the time of Take Over will cause delay. • Missing extinguishers at the time of inspection by authorities = schedule delay • Installation of portable fire extinguishers should be performed in a secure manner so as to ensure that they are still installed at the time of inspection by the authorities- one missing extinguisher can delay the Take Over, and if the certifying/regulatory bodies want to be pedantic, which often is the case, even major milestones like sail away can be delayed. • The above is also applicable to Miscellaneous Safety Equipment • Lack of spares = schedule delay
Safety systems	Passive Fire Protection and Fire Divisions	• Fire doors are notorious for getting damaged during construction and commissioning. Suitable measures must be in place to prevent such damage. If not there will be an impact on the schedule = delay • All fire divisions, penetrations etc., should be inspected and witnessed by the certifying authority prior to the installation of any obscuring "finishings". Removal of false ceilings, wall panels etc. to inspect fire divisions, penetrations etc. = schedule delay

Safety systems	Lifeboats and Life-rafts	• Each lifeboat should be defined as a separate commissioning package, with a dedicated procedure so as to expedite Take Over. A minor problem with one lifeboat could otherwise jeopardize the Take Over of the remaining units = schedule delay • The drop testing or launching of newly installed lifeboats is a requirement of most offshore certifying authorities. However, this can only be performed at the correct operating draft and is weather dependent. The commissioning plan should reflect this and should include all associated tests relative to auxiliary equipment. Re-scheduling or re-testing could quite possibly delay schedule (sail away) • Some of the main equipment, loose equipment and provisions installed inside the lifeboats and life rafts are date stamped and require replacing or re-certification on a regular basis. Failure to have certified equipment= Take over delay = schedule delay.
HVAC	All	• Under-sizing of pressure relief ducting = re-design of airflow=re-commissioning = schedule delay • Use of direct drive fans on high capacity HVAC systems = nonadjustable air volumes = airflow below design = re-design = re commissioning = schedule delay • Undersized heating system to HVAC heating coils = freezing damage= schedule delay • Lack of spares = schedule delay • Lack of operations personnel involved with commissioning = lack of experience and system understanding = commissioning continuously being brought in to show Operations how system work = reduced efficiency and productivity = affecting schedule • Unless commissioned systems have been Taken Over by Operations, they should not be made operational, otherwise commissioning will be responsible for PM = increased commissioning scope = potential schedule delay. • Each HVAC system should be a separate part system/commissioning package with a dedicated procedure. This would enable the commissioned system to be Taken Over in a progressive manner instead of all at the last minute, as would be the case if the total HVAC had to be 100% complete prior to Take Over. The latter = schedule delay

Sub Sea	Topside and subsea part	• Hardware interface responsibility subsea and topside unclear = Poor engineering = schedule delay • Installation of equipment that earlier failed and repaired without determining root cause = Fails after installation subsea = High intervention costs = schedule delay • Lack of integration test of the full subsea "stack up" onshore = late discovery of issues = costly repairs = schedule delay. • Lack of qualification tests of equipment = late modifications = operational limitations on installed equipment= take over issue = schedule delay • Deliveries split between different contract responsibilities = unclear responsibilities on clearing punch items = schedule delay • Small commissioning team = unable to uncover problems early = high workload on team= schedule delay • Unsuitable commissioning support vessels = low contingency due to weather = schedule delay • Lack of ROV support, both technical and equipment = high downtime on ROV = schedule delay • Lack of alignment of control and safety systems philosophies or late completion = Software modifications and commissioning re-testing at-shore + Vendor documentation revisions = affecting schedule • Limited Gateway communications capacity = hardware and software modifications and solution which are not ideal= re-engineering and re-commissioning= schedule delay • Segregation of subsea process and maintenance tags on separate databases = higher complexity for operation and maintenance of system. • Subsea maintenance data not captured in Operation's online Information System= problem with troubleshooting= schedule and Start Up delay • Lack of capacity for future modification = Limited expansion for new wells = New equipment needs to be installed • Lack of On/At-shore pre-testing = changes offshore = schedule delay • Lack of operations personnel involved with commissioning = lack of experience and system understanding = commissioning continuously being brought in to show Operations how system work = reduced efficiency and productivity = affecting schedule • Lack of spares = schedule delay

| General | General | • Lack of clarity of regulators and certifying authorities requirements for witnessing of activities = waste of time = schedule delay.
• Commissioning procedures should be reviewed by the regulatory/ certifying bodies prior to commencing any planned commissioning activities and witness points must clearly be identified in the procedures
• Inadequate communication with regulators and certifying authorities= potential repeat tests = waste of time= schedule delay
• Lack of a formal agreement between regulating bodies as to their involvement in commissioning/ witnessing etc. = waste of time = schedule delay
• Lack of a consistent master register for regulatory/Certifying Auth Issues (put all in PCS) = lack of clarity = waste of time = schedule delay
• Lack of (access to) a regulatory/Certifying Authority advisor = waste of time = schedule delay
• Lack of knowledge on the part of commissioning engineers with regards to national and international mandatory and regulatory requirements= endless discussions (especially with regulators) = waste of time = delays
• Site labor agreement not adequately defined = time consuming process to obtain labor = schedule delay
• Inadequate screening process for design queries = unnecessary changes = schedule delay
• Lack of adverse weather protection = equipment damage, poor work environment = schedule delay
• Inadequate training of commissioning engineers in the use of project standard tools such as PCS, Query register, Punch List process, Work Task System, etc. = waste of time = schedule delay
• Inadequate QA check by Hook Up before hand-over to commissioning (joint punch out should only occur after Hook up's initial QA check) = waste of time = schedule delay
• Lack of complete commissioning procedures prior to start of commissioning = difficult to focus = schedule delay
• Lack of ownership to overall schedule among commissioning engineers = lack of focus = confusion = schedule delay
• Lack of persistency in making Construction completed all work prior to Hand Over to Commissioning = extra work = schedule delay
• Lack of a well defined Take Over procedure at an early phase of the project = endless discussions (with Ops)as to Take Over acceptance criteria = schedule delay
• Lack of Commissioning's review of vendor recommended spares = lack of/wrong spares= schedule delay
• Lack of commissioning follow up of the most important and costly equipment packages from "day one" through to start of commissioning = technical issues = re-engineering = schedule delay. |
| --- | --- | --- |

Risk evaluation

Once you have identified the various risks, you need to categorize these in terms of probability and severity.

Below is a standard but very useful set-up.

Item #	Identified risk	Probability	Severity	Mitigation/ actions	Action by	Deadline
1		High	High			
2		Low	High			
3		Medium	High			
4		High	High			
5		Low	Low			

Concentrate on the High-High's first! You will not have time and resources to cover everything. Remember the 80/20 rule:
20% of the issues causes 80% of the problems

Illustration 59. Risk evaluation matrix

Preparations specifics

In addition to all the various preparations you will have to undertake, there are some very specific items that based on experience, need special attention.

These are:

- Factory Acceptance Testing
- Load Banks for Power Management testing
- N2 Testing of Compressors onshore
- Sub Sea issues
- FPSO specifics

We will discuss these next:

Factory Acceptance Testing

Make sure your system responsible commissioning engineers participate in FAT's Factory Acceptance Testing (FAT). This is very often looked upon as the activity where the design engineer receives his proof of what he specified has been built and actually works.

This is of course very true, and therefore an engineering representative is usually present during the FAT's.

However, it is just as important that a commissioning representative takes part in FAT's, simply because it is a crucial part of understanding how the equipment packages work in order to integrate the package and its associated commissioning procedure in the commissioning activities.

The commissioning engineer has to understand first hand, what deficiencies were discovered during the test, how these were documented (hopefully on a standardized punch list) and what the status of the package documentation including the Operations & Maintenance Manual is.

Not all equipment packages are always subject to FAT's. When that is the case, make sure that Commissioning obtains a complete list of these packages in order for your engineers to evaluate the need for additional testing during commissioning. Also, if for some reason engineering or commissioning does not attend FAT's make sure that you obtain a full list of these, for the same reason as above.

The Use of Load Banks for Power Management Testing

The use of load banks for commissioning of the main generators and the load testing of these (Power Management System) under real life conditions, will under most circumstances require the employment of load bank facilities.

The decision to use a load bank is driven by cost, schedule and the availability of necessary actual load at the time you are supposed to commission the units. Load banks are expensive, and looking solely at costs can prompt the wrong decision.

The schedule part of the decision will, in most cases, promote the rental of a load bank.

It is not practical to commission all of the process systems (that gives you available load) at the same time or in the right sequence (to give you enough load for your power management testing).

As the Main Power Generators always sit on the critical path, you will have to evaluate all the impacts testing without load banks will have on other activities, and again what impact that will have on your critical path activities downstream.

Let's just say it loud and clear before we lose track here: we strongly recommend, for schedule reasons, (and hence for overall cost reasons) to utilize load banks for Power Management Testing. YES, the cost / benefit analysis will in the majority of cases support this decision!

If however, you split the testing between the supplier's work, module site and the integration site you will save money and time. You have resolved the bugs early with the supplier's and / or module yard, and you require less testing at the integration site.

The testing at the supplier's should be covered by the original purchase order!

Nitrogen (N^2) Test-Run of Gas Compressor Trains Onshore

In areas of the world where strict flaring limitations are imposed (now in most parts of the industrialized world), and / or where offshore Personnel Onboard (POB) is limited, the benefit of performing a full run test of the gas compressors on Nitrogen is unquestionably a huge benefit. The savings in offshore hours are tremendous as all major trouble shooting, repairs and control settings are done onshore. Typically, these are the areas where you save time and money

- It will be the first time the compression system is operating as an integral part of its designated process system and has to interact with the process control system
- Several of the process control parameters and parameters in the unit's own control system can be set during these tests. That saves a lot of compressor start-up time and process tuning offshore.
- Weaknesses and faults in equipment and control systems are often detected through these tests, and there is still time to get replacement parts and make necessary

modifications without having an impact on the start-up date for oil production and gas injection.

- It will be the first time the electrical drive motors (where applicable) or turbines and compressor auxiliaries are fully hooked up to the platform (electrical) system.
- It will be the first time the units are run on load (as FAT's are normally no-load string tests).
- The rotor dynamic performance of the compressor units is verified onshore under high load conditions. It is usually high vibration levels or bearing temperatures that are showing up during these test conditions and these can obviously be more easily handled onshore than offshore.

All these factors will contribute to the likelihood of problems surfacing, being resolved and modifications being implemented, particularly in control systems. Several vendor representatives will have to be called in to help resolve the issues, which is not a great concern onshore, but would have been offshore relative to POB and cost. It should be noted that this testing scenario is becoming a best practice activity in the industry.

The general experience is that the order of 10-12 weeks in offshore start-up time of the gas compression system is saved by performing the run tests during the onshore phase, at the module yard or at the integration site (depending on system configuration and lay-out).

Normally this also has a significant effect on oil production during the initial offshore phase, because of the flaring restriction. Production will have to be cut back when the associated gas is being flared rather than injected. The cost impact in terms of additional direct costs is related to having a significant number of vendor personnel and commissioning personnel on rotation for extended periods, as well as the additional logistic costs for material and personnel.

Experience figures indicate that the cost of offshore hours is slightly more than 3 times the cost of onshore hours.

So, if your project falls in the category of strict flaring limitations or very restricted offshore POB, you should prepare for running the gas compressors on N^2 during the onshore /at shore phase.

Sub-Sea Related Issues

In dealing with a subsea project with topsides interfaces, there are several areas that require your attention. As explained in the value chain discussions previously, the biggest value loss is always in the interfaces. This is particularly true for subsea / topsides interfaces. These are some very important interface issues to consider:

- Ensure that the whole Project Team and the main contractors understand the subsea commissioning requirements at an early stage of the project.
- Ensure that the work scope of the contractors interfacing with subsea has a clear scope of work and clear inter-contractor interfaces.
- Align the Control and Safety philosophies early and maintain consistency, subsea and topsides
- Align software development and delivery to match the commissioning schedule to avoid re-testing and re-commissioning.
- Check topsides-to-sub-sea gateway communications as early as possible by simulations, to make sure there are no problems and potential schedule impact.
- Integrate sub-sea data into topsides database, capturing systems and standardizing formats, including data warehousing and maintenance systems etc.
- Ensure sub-sea control and support systems mounted topsides are designed for expansions to meet sub-sea needs.
- Carry out full comprehensive testing of topsides sub-sea equipment as early as possible onshore, to disclose issues and minimize costly offshore testing.
- Carry out full comprehensive FAT's and Site Integration Test (stack-up test) of sub-sea equipment onshore, with experienced client personnel in attendance.
- Ensure that there is a clear responsibility split between topsides and sub-sea and that all gaps are closed.
- Ensure deliverables from multi-suppliers and contractors are clear and check for gaps in responsibilities and ownership.

FPSO Specific Considerations

Although the majority of the contents of this book are relevant to any project, whether it is a Gravity Base Structure (GBS), a Steel Jacket (SJ), a Floating Production Unit (FPU), a Floating Production Storage and Offloading Unit (FPSO) or others, there are some very specific considerations that should be given to the commissioning of an FPSO.

Most of the FPSO specifics are basically "straight forward" system commissioning, like ballast water, station keeping systems, thrusters and associated systems, winch systems and cargo-handling systems. These systems not normally found on other offshore installations. The only real issue you have to look for here is making sure the vessel systems, if designed to supply the Topsides systems, have sufficient capacity to do so. Make sure you incorporate activities for re-commissioning of these systems once they are hooked up to the Topsides systems.

These systems are not more difficult to commission than other systems, but because the hull of an FPSO is considered a ship, you have the added complexity of interfacing with and satisfying the class responsible entity (Lloyds/Veritas or others) of all activities considered "class" and any changes you might make to "class" systems.

It is, however, one very specific piece of equipment that is truly unique to an FPSO; the Turret, and that requires very dedicated and professional attention. The Turret and mooring systems of an FPSO represent some unique challenges to commissioning. Whether internal (mounted a top vessel moon pool) or external (mounted externally to vessel bow), it functions as the connection point of the vessel to the seabed. All gas, water, process and utility fluid that must have communication to sub-sea must pass through the turret, effectively concentrating some aspect of nearly every FPSO system on the turret. Aside from diversity, the turret becomes a special consideration due to the necessity of having one part stationary with the earth, and one part rotational with the FPSO. This adds a level of complexity to each system passing through the turret and becomes even more complex if the turret has mooring system disconnection capability.

The following pages discuss the most important issues that need to be focused on in the planning/preparations and execution phase on an FPSO/Turret-project. Because the Turret is such a unique feature, we have for clarity reasons, provided some additional technical descriptions.

The most important areas to focus during the planning/preparations phase (as well as the execution phase) in regards to the turret are:

- A thorough review of specifications and design details of packaged items to ensure the requirements for Factory Acceptance Testing are aligned with and meet the expectations of the overall commissioning program.

- A coordinated approach with the turret contractor to defining the system boundary limits and determination of when (i.e. onshore / at shore/in shore / offshore) in the assembly program components and systems can be commissioned.

- A thorough review of the interface areas between topsides, turret and sub-sea systems to ensure the commissioning performed on each is complementary, meets the expectations of the project commissioning philosophy, and will result in a seamless transition to system hand over at project close-out.

- Analysis involving the turret contractor to review static and dynamic commissioning man-hours to ensure such factors as space constraints, unique components, lessons learned, and details specific to the current design are taken into consideration.

- Preparation and review of commissioning procedures by personnel from the turret contractor and the client to ensure unique systems are properly tested at the correct time, that adequate preservation routines are specified, and that commissioning spares are identified and purchased. An added benefit that will be eschewed from this approach is that the client's expectations will become better defined and well understood.

- Quality Control vigilance on preservation for turret interface areas, tubing and pipe work in particular, that remains exposed until final module hookup. Monitoring by the turret contractor of hook-up activities in the stationary-to-rotational turret interfaces.

- Commissioning team attendance and acceptance of Factory Acceptance Testing.

- Inclusion of turret expertise on the commissioning team, in particular for areas of unique turret specific systems such as the swivels or disconnection capability.

- Identification and mobilization of key vendors for specialized turret equipment.

- That effective communication exists among the turret, topsides, sub-sea; vessel commissioning personnel and that adequate resource are applied at the correct time for turret system testing.

Turret Swivels

Fluid swivels are a necessary component to allow the rotating pipework of the vessel to connect with the stationary pipework of the turret. Swivels may vary in size, flow rate and pressure rating capability but they share some common attributes and some unique ones as well. A means of facilitating low friction rotation, normally through utilization of integral roller bearings is common. Such a system requires lubrication from an external dedicated source.

The sealing system of fluid swivels can be either passive or active. Passive seals contain the process fluids within the swivel annulus without external influence. An active sealing system utilizes a buffer fluid, which is externally applied via a dedicated hydraulic power unit to the swivel. The buffer fluid is maintained in the outer sealed ring of the swivel at a higher pressure than the inner process fluid. Used mainly for higher-pressure applications or for compressible media (gas), this method effectively prevents escape of the process fluid to atmosphere.

Additionally swivels normally will allow some passage of fluid to move over the seals either because of design (to aid in lubrication) or because of wear. In these cases, a leak detection and recovery system is utilized to monitor, collect and dispose of the fluid.

Turret Electrical and Instrumentation

Although not unique in the application to the turret, there are two aspects that deserve attention.

The swivel system to carry electrical power normally utilizes slip rings and is in most cases not field serviceable. Attention must be made to performing comprehensive factory acceptance testing so as to minimize and eliminate as much field commissioning as possible.

Control signals may be hardwired via slip rings as well, or they may be transferred via an optical swivel. Again the emphasis on factory acceptance testing is essential, but so is due care and diligence during installation at the vessel assembly yard.

The cost of swivel signal paths versus the sheer amount of data to be sent to the vessel distributed control system most often results in marshalling part of this system on the turret. It is not uncommon for 25 to 40% of total vessel I/O to reside wholly on the turret in an autonomous distributed control system with its own logic and software to control turret and sub-sea functions.

This aspect of commissioning is not normally thought of with respect to a turret and often accounts for significant commissioning man-hours. With the concentration of space on a turret, care must be taken to ensure proper signal shielding and adherence to code limitations as well. Often, the results of failure in this area only become apparent during final dynamic commissioning.

Disconnect-ability

In harsh environmental areas, especially in iceberg alleys in northern areas, FPSOs are designed to be disconnect- able by means of the lower turret being connected to a subsurface moored buoy via disconnect-able valves and controls.

The addition of disconnect capability will add to the complexity of nearly every system on the turret. In simple terms, each connection to sub-sea will incorporate a means to release itself either in tandem with all others, or in sequence. A dedicated control system with dedicated mechanical field devices to initiate release will be present. All process, water, gas and utility systems will incorporate modified shutdown sequences to prepare for disconnection.

Additionally, the FPSO vessel control system will also carry additional features to control vessel movement before, during and after disconnection.

Commissioning of these systems will be a multi-disciplined effort and will require the services of a commissioning engineer inherently familiar with the design, manufacture and operation of the disconnect components.

Turret Construction and Assembly

Internal turrets are normally constructed in an upper and lower module, with the schedule for the lower portion heavily driven by the vessel construction or refit critical path. This will limit the time available for fabrication yard outfitting and commissioning of systems resident in this portion of the module. External turrets are somewhat less sensitive to this constraint. In general, the interface areas of the turret will be from turret to sub-sea, turret to turret (i.e. upper to lower), turret to vessel (mainly structural) and turret to topsides.

Careful attention must be made to the preservation of cables, piping, tubing and other components that are subjected to interruption at these interface points. The application of hot oil flushing must be well thought out, as the amount of interface interruptions may negate the advantage of pre-hook-up cleaning of these items.

To some extent, the amount of interface points at the turret will affect the timing of commissioning of the associated systems. In some instances it may not be possible to commission systems piecemeal or it may be of limited benefit to undertake work prior to hook-up completion.

Integration and communication among the topsides, turret, and sub-sea commissioning personnel is essential to ensure the program developed achieves the maximum benefit in line with project goals. Attention by the turret contractor of hook-up activities in the stationary-to-rotational turret interfaces is recommended. Clashes that will appear only when the vessel rotates may not be apparent to the untrained eye. By the same token, attention should be made to the placement of commissioning and construction temporaries, including power sources and resulting cables or pipes.

FPSO general

There are several other issues experienced with FPSOs that should be noticed. The FPSO hull and utility systems are normally designed according to "ship standard" and classification requirements. That means the systems are made to be maintained and often overhauled periodically requiring docking of the ship/hull. However, that will normally not be the case for an FPSO since it is supposed to operate on a 24/7 basis year in and year out. One of the main issues is corrosion, both surface corrosion and corrosion under insulation. A lot of the ship utility and cargo systems are designed with use of standard carbon steel material, galvanized piping, and use of brass and copper material, often heavily exposed to green sea and/or to a humid, salty and corrosive atmosphere. The selection of the poor material quality for piping and equipment is therefore a challenge, especially for the Operations team. A coating program should definitely be on the agenda for such systems.

The second main issue that will be a challenge for both Commissioning and Operations is the ship piping systems design. Most of the ship piping systems are very often lacking enough piping isolation valves and block and bleed arrangements due their "ship" design.

The third main issue is about the piping lay out and flexibility of the piping runs. A FPSO is moving a lot that will impact and move the piping systems both sideways and lengthwise. A good designer will normally put in expansion loops to cater for this. However, this is normally not the case and the piping systems are often provided with f. ex. "Straub couplings" to compensate for the lengthwise movements. Over time these couplings often start to leak due to the movement and wear, causing environmental spill challenges.

The issues are not all directly linked to commissioning, however when Commissioning reviews design for commissioning-ability the points above should be considered.

SUMMARY-Key Success Factors in the Preparation phase

✓ Make sure everybody understands the value chain concept and the internal customer/supplier relationships in the organization.

✓ Do not blend Construction and Commissioning departments into one entity.

✓ Build an organization with continuity from module yard to integration yard in mind.

✓ Make sure your lead personnel are recruited in the early engineering phase.

✓ Don't be impressed by CV's. Check credentials.

✓ Involve Operations personnel early. Recruit them into responsible positions.

✓ At integration site, initiate a task force based (process oriented) organizational structure with all project departments, Operations included in order to drive the Take-Overs.

✓ Make sure Commissioning has dedicated labor pools to draw from.

✓ Regardless of contractual model, make sure you audit the commissioning organization/processes.

✓ Instigate risk analysis sessions. At least perform one in the module yard phase, one before integration, one midway through integration and one prior to starting the offshore phase.

✓ Rigorously follow up all prioritized actions from the risk analysis sessions. Involve the engineering department early.

✓ Make sure a thorough spares review has been performed.

✓ Make sure all contracts for tools, equipment and temporaries are in place.

✓ Make sure commissioning participates in the factory acceptance testing of the main equipment packages.

✓ Hire a load bank for the power management testing.

✓ Prepare for a full test of the compressor trains on Nitrogen onshore.

✓ Prepare for a full onshore simulation test of the subsea system including all interfaces with topsides.

✓ Prepare for full onshore integration test of turret systems with topsides systems.

3.0 EXECUTION

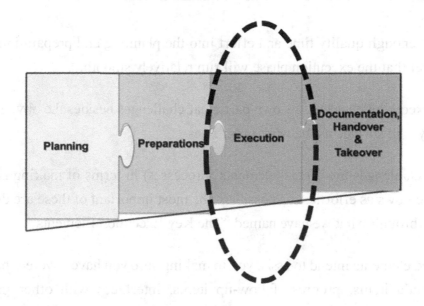

- The Key Execution Elements
- Monitoring and improving the plan
- Execution specifics
- Critical execution activities and associated schedule impact- "The BIG 7"
- Summary: Key Success Factors in the Execution phase

The crucial part of any successful schedule execution is the actions you take after the plan is created!

In this chapter we will be discussing important elements of the execution phase such as "the Key Execution Elements, monitoring and improving the plan and critical path analysis. We will also discuss loop testing, system cleanliness, hot oil flushing, sub-sea simulation testing, preservation issues, onshore N^2- testing of compressors, timing of the installation of process control valves and pressure relief valves, subsea system integration testing, and the potential effect these activities may have on the overall schedule.

The Key Execution Elements

If you have put enough quality time and effort into the planning and preparations phases, it is our firm belief that the execution phase will run relatively smooth.

However, the execution phase has its own particular challenges besides the obvious technical ones that surely will surface as the work progresses.

Some of these challenges are crucial elements (processes) in terms of making sure that the execution phase flows as effortless as possible. The most important of these are described on the next pages through what we have named "The Key Execution Elements"

These described elements intend to assist you in making sure you have covered the necessary processes, agenda items, progress follow-up items, interfaces with other groups, info distribution etc.

It is intended to be a "reminder list", and will obviously not cover all project specific items necessary for the execution of all projects.

These " Key Execution Elements" are described on the next pages.

Execution elements describe the processes or items that you need particular focus on, and are pieces of a puzzle that must come together in order to secure an efficient and streamlined execution.

Below are the Key Execution Elements.

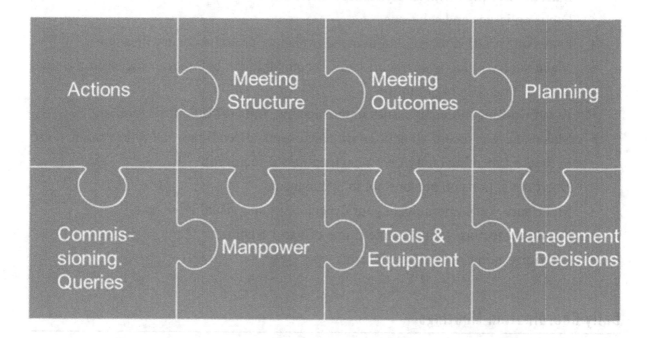

Illustration 60. The Key Execution Elements

Meeting Structure

You need to device a meeting structure that supports the execution follow up.

A meaningful meeting structure can be an excellent tool to streamline the execution process. It can also be an excellent way of wasting everybody's time.

When you design the meeting structure and agendas, the following are some useful guidelines that should assist you in streamlining meetings:

Weekly Meetings

This meeting is primarily used to discuss overall progress and related issues. The following should be considered.

- Invite only direct reports (line and staff), plus materials contact person (if not direct report). (Let the Leads hold meetings with their direct reports as and when required).

- It is useful to have a senior Operations representative in attendance.
- Start all meetings with safety issues / information
- Focus on issues and solutions.
- Focus on variation to the plan-demand explanations and recovery measures.
- Make sure you focus on each Lead's accountabilities before you focus on the total picture. This fosters discipline.
- Avoid working too many issues in the meeting. Initiate "off-lines" for that.
- Make sure you record all actions with actionee and deadlines and follow up on these in the next meeting (and in between meetings if required).
- Don't put actions on persons not in attendance
- Make sure you communicate your expectations and visualize results.
- Keep the meeting within a time frame of 1 to 1.5 hours.
- Distribute minutes to all participants

Daily Coordination Meetings

These meetings should be used only to discuss practical issues that are or can impede the progress. Attendees would be basically the same as for the weekly meeting.

- Discuss today's *upcoming activities* and required inter-leads or inter-project coordination activities (personnel, materials, etc.).
- In addition to the "standard" attendance, it is recommended to have the Certifying Authority (e.g. Veritas/Lloyds Register) attending to keep them up to speed on issues, so as to avoid hold ups based on delayed information.
- You should use this meeting to screen Commissioning Queries (remove the "nice to haves") to avoid overloading the engineering system.
- Keep the meeting to a maximum of one hour.

Other Regular Meetings

These will obviously vary with projects and project phases. Initially, these meetings will be held separately, but as the project progresses, it is advisable to combine the meetings (except the inter-project management meeting) in a "task force" meeting structure as described in the organizations chapter herein.

Meeting Outcomes

Here you should specifically look for systemic issues that repeatedly come out of each meeting. If you find systemic issues, you can suspect that your processes are not working satisfactorily and / or you have common equipment / material quality issues that need to be resolved, or even organizational issues that need require attention.

When it comes to meeting outcomes, your expectations should be along the lines below:

- Progress issues that need to be processed, either in the form of simple actions or in the form of a more formal process, such as management approval and/or schedule change process.
- Resource issues; these can be anything from labor call off process not working satisfactory and to filling vacant engineer positions, etc.
- Material issues that need to be actioned. If systemic, check process.
- Equipment failures that need rectification. Here you should be asking for common symptoms or inherent equipment issues that need further investigation.
- Vendor attendance issues. You should be looking for variations, or confirmation that you do not have issues here that can jeopardize the schedule. Check call-off process and contracts for gaps.
- Are there issues outside of the commissioning organization that need to be resolved? If systemic, call a management meeting to discuss with relevant parties.
- Are there issues inside of the commissioning organization that need to be resolved? If systemic, discuss with relevant parties.
- Check the trend on Queries for systemic issues and / or check if screening process is working adequately.
- Number of Punch Lists items raised should give you a good indication of quality of equipment, quality at hand-over from Construction and / or quality of systems handed over to Operations. If trend shows increased number of Punch List items, check Construction quality process and / or your own quality checks prior to take- over by Operations.
- Check if there are issues with temporary equipment, check suppliers and contracts.
- Check if there are issues with preservation.

Planning

The weekly progress reporting is one of the most important parts of the project execution circle. The timing of and the amount of time lead engineers have to spend in completing the process is critical. Having shown the numbers of different reports that need to be produced to enable you as a manager to pin point the areas of concern, it is of the utmost importance that your reports are accurate and on time.

With this in mind, the "planning department" (planner) has to have the progress input report distributed to the lead engineers in sufficient time for accurate progressing and prior to the agreed progress shut off.

This report is precise; each engineer knows what needs to be reported and when the report is returned to planning.

Remember the timing here is critical for the turnaround of the reports. The progress curve and the leads' curve in general are the ones everyone is looking for early! The results of the week's progress will be high-lighted in the following reports:

- Bean Count
- Lead Charts
- Score Cards
- Tracking Sheets (including Vendors)
- Progress Curves

The full picture will not be ready until the progress has been input into the network, time now set and the total network analyzed with new changes included. This is where your experienced planning engineer comes into action, maintaining the schedule completion date, keeping the critical path on line, not impacting the manning levels too significantly and looking for improvements.

It is vital, that you, as the manager, realize that this is not about data manipulation to keep the dates you would like to see, but about visualizing the truth!

Commissioning Queries

The greatest growth contribution on a typical project stems from Queries. It is extremely important that the Query process is sound and that an adequate screening is in place within commissioning. You don't want to overload the system with "unnecessary" Queries.

Once you have raised a Query, all you want to do is follow-up on the process to ensure that the Query is not affecting the schedule. It is sometimes too easy to blame Engineering for hold ups when it comes to Queries. Quite often you will find that the initiator, the Commissioning engineer, has not read the response from Engineering in order to OK it or not, hence Commissioning is holding it up, or the initial Query description made by Commissioning was not clear and concise enough for engineering to decipher.

So, check the whole process, not just parts of it!

Your follow up should include:

- Quantity identified
- Quantity with Engineering
- Quantity Outstanding - with Engineering or initiator
- Quantity on hold and reasons
- Schedule risk evaluation

The Engineering Query report should give you all the above data (with the exception of the schedule risk evaluation); however, a report is just a piece of paper. It is your persistent follow-up that makes it come alive and become a useful tool for everyone. Below is a typical Query format.

Typical Query Format

Commissioning Query Form			
Query Number CQ -		Date Issued	
Title		Requires	Y/N
Title:		Engineering	:-_____
		Spares	:-_____
Prepared by Name	Date	Documentation	:-_____
		Vendor Supt	:-_____
Approved by: Name	Date	Matl. Delivery	:-_____
		Other	:-_____
Query sent to: Name	Date		
Description of Query			
Project Response			
Prepared by	Name:	Date:	
Approved By	Name:	Date:	
Operations Review		Date:	
Responsible accepted		Date:	

The purpose of this form is to describe any technical queries which arise during the Pre-commissioning and commissioning work of the Project.

This form is used to by all personell involved with any part of the Commissioning scope and should cover all technical questions/problems arising during the commissioning of syhstems. The documentation of these queries and their solutions will form an important part of the data history for the system. All responses must be strictley adhered to. The attached flow chart shows the path the query will follow.

Illustration 61. Typical Query Format

Below is a typical Query Handling process.

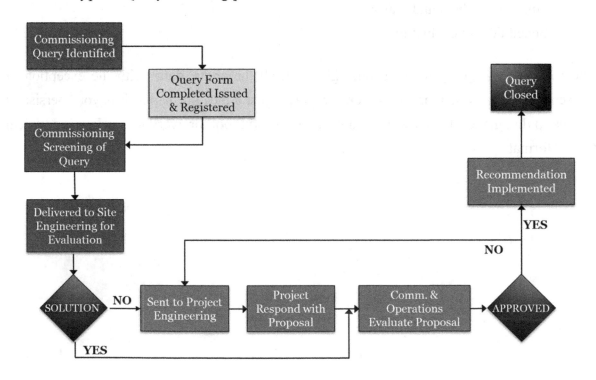

Illustration 62. Process for handling of Commissioning Queries

Manpower Requirements

To enable the Lead Engineers to produce accurate manpower requirement levels, the weekly labor demand sheet is created. The planner first produces the 6-week look-ahead schedule from the network and next prints out the Lead Engineers manpower histogram. The manning numbers are in turn transferred to the weekly labor demand sheets. Each Lead then assesses if the requirements are correct and decides if more or less manpower is required.

Once this exercise is complete, the required assistance numbers are transmitted to the Contractor for implementation. Under normal execution conditions, these numbers would be discussed once a week at a joint Construction / Commissioning meeting. The actual supplied manpower figures given at the meeting will then be added each week to the Labor demand sheet completing the circle. If shortfalls are encountered, a report will be transmitted to the Contractor requesting additional manpower supplies for commissioning.

The Vendor mobilization is controlled by means of the vendor call-out schedule and coordinated at a single focal point, namely the Vendor Coordinator. Make sure your process is in order to avoid vendor call-outs from "whoever" feels like it. This will save you time, money and frustrations.

Below is a typical Weekly labor demand sheet.

Manpower Requirements

Project - Weekley Labour Demand

Date: 01.07.2014

Directs

	Current 01.07.2014		Week Ending 08.07.2014		Week Ending 15.07.2014		Week Ending 22.07.2014		Week Ending 29.07.2014		Week Ending 05.08.2014		Week Ending 12.08.2014		Week Ending 19.08.2014		Good Friday Saturday	
	Reqd	Actual	Reqd	Actual	Reqd	Actual	Reqd	Actual	Reqd	Actual	Reqd	Actual	Reqd	Actual	Reqd	Actual	Reqd	Actual
Process Lead																		
Piping	6	6	6		6		6		6		6		6		6		6	
Millwrights	6	5	6		6		6		6		6		6		6		6	
Boiler Makers																		
Totals	12	11	12	0	12	0	12	0	12	0	12	0	12	0	12	0	12	0
Electrical Lead																		
Electricians	19	19	19		19		19		19		19		19		19		19	
Insulators	1	1	1		1		1		1		1		1		1		1	
Totals	20	20	20	0	20	0	20	0	20	0	20	0	20	0	20	0	20	0
Instrument Lead																		
Inst. Piping (Inst. Tech)	6	6	6		6		6		6		6		6		6		6	
Electricians (Inst. Tech)	8	8	8		8		8		8		8		8		8		8	
Totals	14	14	14	0	14	0	14	0	14	0	14	0	14	0	14	0	14	0
Vessel Lead																		
Millwrights	2	2	2		2		2		2		2		2		2		2	
Totals	2	2	2	0	2	0	2	0	2	0	2	0	2	0	2	0	2	0
Preservation																		
Piping	3	4	3		3		3		3		3		3		3		3	
Sheet Metal	1	1	1		1		1		1		1		1		1		1	
Millwrights	6	6	6		6		6		6		6		6		6		6	
Totals	10	11	10	0	10	0	10	0	10	0	10	0	10	0	10	0	10	0

Illustration 63. Typical weekly labor demand sheet

Tools and Equipment

The timely availability of tools and equipment is obviously of utmost importance for the progress of the work. Once the contracts for the supply of tools and equipment are in place, you need to monitor the performance of these contracts during the execution phase.

Not only do you need to check the contracts for supply of standard tools and equipment, but you also need to monitor deficiencies relative to critical items delivery.

Yes, the Materials group will do this for you, but nonetheless, you need to check the on-site delivery dates relative to the commissioning schedule. It is your input that makes up the Materials group's critical items delivery list and forms the basis for the expediting of these items.

It is considered sound practice to have one single point of contact with respect to materials working closely with the Commissioning Team. Preferable this contact should participate in all regular commissioning meetings (as explained under "meeting structure"), thereby you have a daily interface with Materials Control.

Make sure you use the materials contact person for ALL material issues, whether it is materials via the hook-up contractor, local suppliers, remote suppliers, bulk material controls at site, vendor package spares or others.

Also make sure your engineers forward damage reports to the Materials contact person for distribution and follow-up with suppliers.

Management Decisions

Make sure you push decision-making as far down the line as practical!

You, as the manager, do not want to be a bottleneck in the system. There is, for example, no sense in you approving every Purchase Order issued by Commissioning. Design a simple authorization matrix that defines levels of approval and distribute to all team members.

Remember to distribute this also to other project members such as Materials Control, Engineering, Construction, etc.

In this way you save time and avoid a lot of frustrated people trying to find you to sign a minor purchase order.

This authorization matrix should at least cover items such as:

- Spending levels
- Budget changes
- Schedule changes-minor/major
- Query approvals (commissioning screening of Queries)
- Contracts accountabilities
- Mobilization of manpower

Actions

An action is not an action if not accompanied by an accountable and a deadline!

Make sure you communicate your expectations to the team when it comes to actions.

You should make it clear and demonstrate that all actions will be followed up rigorously.

Unless valid excuses are produced, you will not accept overdue actions.

Also, make sure that all action items accountable, deadline and results are communicated to relevant personnel. Quite often, one person's actions have bearings on another person's ability to perform his / hers job. For example, if you don't make sure that actions are liquidated, you will find a cascading effect that has greater impact than the single action itself. This is where you start running into problems.

Therefore, the timely execution of actions is a must on the project.

Remember, not only is it important that your personnel liquidate actions in a timely fashion, but also that YOU do the same. Your whole team might be held up awaiting your actions!

LEAD BY EXAMPLE!

Monitoring and Improving the Plan

This subject could have been presented in the Planning section of the book. However, as the monitoring and improving of the plan is a key activity during execution, we have chosen to present it here.

A specific project in this business is unique, a one-time endeavor with a start, a finish and generally a strict budget. Selected people will execute the project, who may have never worked together before in a team of such magnitude and at different locations. At the initial concept, the Project Manager has to think what he/she needs to accomplish, what steps are needed, who needs to carry out the steps and how to keep the **_SPIRITS UP?_**

- ✓ **Selected**
- ✓ **People**
- ✓ **Included**
- ✓ **Really**
- ✓ **Inspire**
- ✓ **The**
- ✓ **Success**
- ✓ **Upon**
- ✓ **Projects**

= _spirits up_

Successful project management requires dedication and constant vigilance in terms of what has actually happened, what was actually accomplished, what remains to be completed and what resources are available to do it. Contingency plans must be in place that handles day to day problems which occur while running the project, some of which are covered in this book.

Project Managers will have a good understanding of the processes involved to reach the goals of the project; however, they should also recognize the steps for updating, incorporating change or adjusting existing methodology during the project, i.e. - improvements!

The aim is always to improve the schedule in a continuous improvement cycle. The key elements that should be considered when making improvement decisions are:

- Planning
- Measuring & Controlling
- Improvement and Administration

These are described next.

The illustration below describes the Key Improvement Cycle and Decision Points

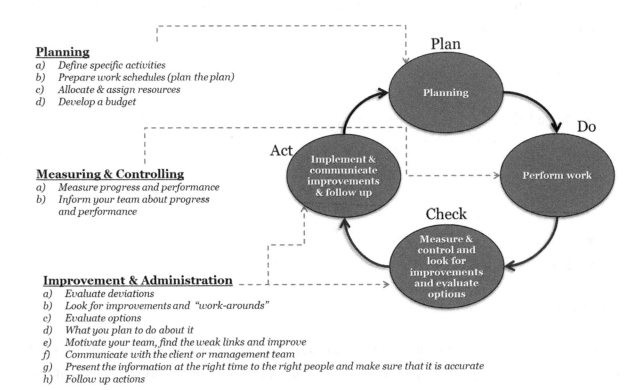

Planning
a)   *Define specific activities*
b)   *Prepare work schedules (plan the plan)*
c)   *Allocate & assign resources*
d)   *Develop a budget*

Measuring & Controlling
a)   *Measure progress and performance*
b)   *Inform your team about progress and performance*

Improvement & Administration
a)   *Evaluate deviations*
b)   *Look for improvements and "work-arounds"*
c)   *Evaluate options*
d)   *What you plan to do about it*
e)   *Motivate your team, find the weak links and improve*
f)   *Communicate with the client or management team*
g)   *Present the information at the right time to the right people and make sure that it is accurate*
h)   *Follow up actions*

Illustration 64. The Key Improvement Cycle and decision Points

Critical Path Analysis

Plan the work, and work the plan!

There is not much point in spending months and months on planning the work, just to find out that when it comes to executing the work, the plan is forgotten and the work is all over the place.

You as the manager need to make sure that the plan is being used as the main tool to steer and monitor the work. You have to make sure that all your lead personnel understand that working on the critical activities is the key to success. The only way to make sure this happens is to constantly monitor the critical path of the plan and to visualize this in every status /progress meeting you have with your Leads.

Every time the plan is adjusted or revised, you must keep the critical path highlighted in all dealings with your leads and engineers to make sure you stay on it.

Review the critical path with your planner, review the actual work progressed so far and find out if there are deviations. Highlight the deviations, demand explanations from your Leads and get back on track, or revise the plan.

Review the critical path in every regular status meetings and TALK ABOUT IT!

This is a simple and effective way to monitor the critical path activities on a frequent basis and to make sure your organization is focused.

Execution specifics

This section deals with some very important technical execution specific issues that empirically represent significant threats to the execution program.

These are:

- Loop Testing
- Preservation
- Piping cleanliness
- N^2 Testing of Compressors
- Oil Flushing
- Sub Sea simulation testing
- SIT testing of subsea equipment
- Timing of the installation of Main Control Valves and Pressure Relief Valves

Loop Testing

The loop testing generally falls into two distinct phases within commissioning; the "Loop Function Test" and the "Final Loop Function Test."

The loop function test is to be considered the Pre-Commissioning part where the objectives are:

- Verify suppliers / manufactures calibration.
- Expose any defective loop components.
- Verify loop functions and continuity.
- Reveal any hidden outstanding Mechanical Completion Scope.
- Uncover deviations with respect to calibrations (instruments shall be re-calibrated, repaired or replaced if defective).

The final loop function test and any consequent calibration will be carried out prior to final commissioning when the loops are complete. Before the loop testing starts ensure that all necessary documentation is available. The following list is a guide to the minimum documentation required:

- Loop drawings.
- Instrument Data sheets -matched with P & ID's.
- Instrument index.
- System configuration index.

Loop test timing should coincide with the final installation of Control Valves.

The following attachments are guidelines as to the Loop Testing scope and break points between Mechanical Completion and the Commissioning Scope.

Loop Function Test Nomenclature

Loop from instrument junction box. "Field-limited Loop Function Test"

When there is no multi-core between junction box and cross wiring cabinet, the loop may be powered in the junction box and tested to this. The purpose of performing a preliminary loop function test will be to identify instruments requiring recalibration and to check field cable continuity.

This work should be carried out in mechanical completion.

Below is a typical Field-limited Loop Function Test Lay Out

Typical Field- limited Loop Function Test Lay Out

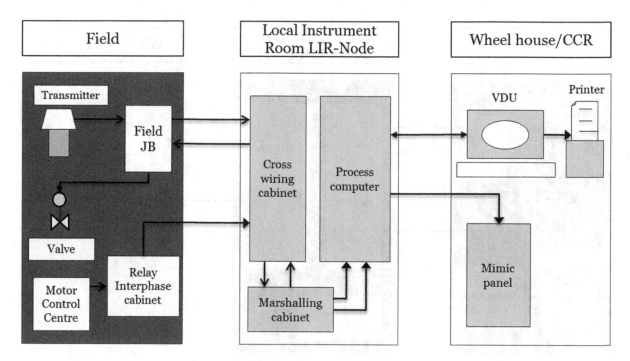

Illustration 65. Typical Field limited Loop Testing Lay out

Loop from instrument to cross wiring cabinet –"Loop Function Test"

When there is no connection between the cross wiring cabinet and the control room, the loop is tested to the cross wiring cabinet. Loops are often powered in the cross wiring cabinet, otherwise the loop has to be powered with external power supply in the cross wiring cabinet. Care must be taken when performing this scope. If mechanical completion is not totally complete, a full safety analysis should be performed.

Local loop

This may be a loop from the instrument to a vendor skid. The loop test should be performed when the skid is powered up. A local pneumatic loop may be fully tested when the installation is complete.

This work should be carried out in pre-commissioning

Below is a typical Loop Function Test Lay Out

Typical Loop Function Test Lay Out

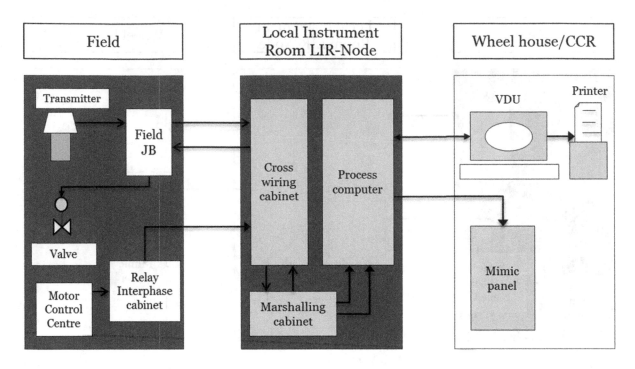

Illustration 66. Typical Loop Function Test Lay Out

Loop from instrument to control room (CCR or Wheel house)"Final Loop Instrument Function Test"

This is the full loop and may be tested close up to normal operating conditions. The loop is powered and signals are received to and transmitted from the control room.

This work should be carried out in commissioning

Below is a typical Final Loop Function Test Lay Out

Typical Final Loop Function Test Lay Out

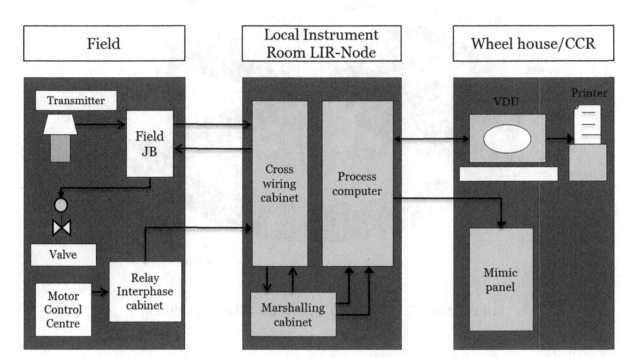

Illustration 67. Typical Final Loop Function Test Lay Out

Critical execution activities and associated schedule impact - "The BIG 7"

Empirically there are some activities that have the potential to impact the schedule more than others in the execution phase, and hence are schedule-critical activities that require special attention in this phase. Obviously there are many other execution activities that will, unless due care is taken, cause schedule impact, but the ones described herein are in our experience the "big ticket items"

We have defined these as "The big 7" and these are all explained on the following pages.

The illustration below shows the overall distribution of the schedule delay potential relative to "the Big 7". The whole pie chart makes up the total schedule delay potential (100%) attributed to the various elements discussed next.

The overall distribution of the schedule delay potential relative to the Big 7:

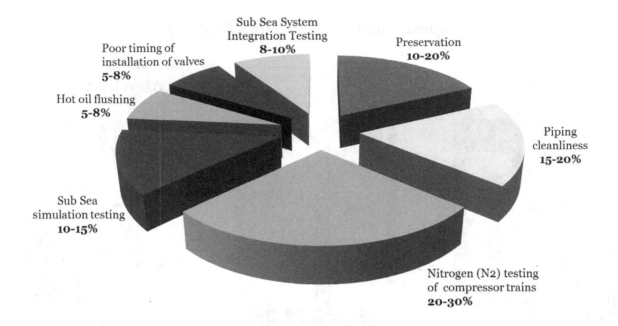

Illustration 68. "The Big 7"- schedule delay distribution

Preservation

Lack of proper preservation routines can be extremely costly.

It is an area that is notoriously overlooked and projects are paying dearly time and time again.

Typically on a multi-module project, the overall schedule delay caused by lack of early preservation can be as high as 8-12 weeks and the dollar value is typically in six digit numbers.

You have to make sure you establish a preservation program that starts running at the module yards and continues through integration and pre-start up.

The most efficient way to make sure you are covered in this important area is to recruit a Preservation Engineer on the project as soon as the major equipment packages have been installed. The Preservation Engineer should (must!) report to Commissioning (and not to Construction). You as the Commissioning Manager will have to live with any wrong doings, so make sure you have maximum influence!

Make sure the person you employ is familiar with the project requirements and have this person develop the preservation program.

This is an area where it would be very beneficial to employ a person from the Operations Department, who will feel ownership to the equipment, as he/she will have to live with it for many years to come.

Don't only base the preservation program on the package vendor recommendations!

The equipment outside the vendor packages comprises a very large portion of the equipment needing attention.

Experience also tells us that lack of preservation in the warehouses can be quite detrimental to the job. So make sure your preservation engineer audits, and if necessary, educates the warehouse personnel when it comes to correct storage and handling of sensitive parts, like machine parts, electronics, etc.

The illustration below shows the empirical value of the *Preservation* schedule impact potential.

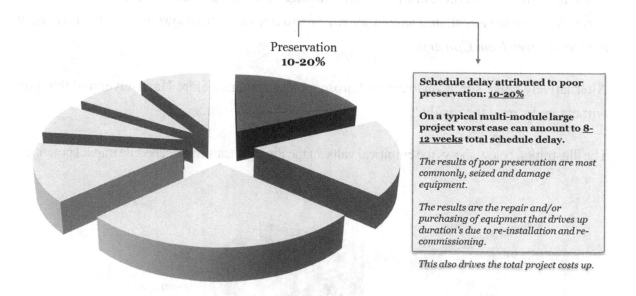

**Preservation
10-20%**

Schedule delay attributed to poor preservation: <u>10-20%</u>

On a typical multi-module large project worst case can amount to <u>8-12 weeks</u> total schedule delay.

The results of poor preservation are most commonly, seized and damage equipment.

The results are the repair and/or purchasing of equipment that drives up duration's due to re-installation and re-commissioning.

This also drives the total project costs up.

Illustration 69. Poor Preservation-schedule impact potential

Piping Cleanliness

Piping cleanliness is a major issue in the commissioning of any system, but never more important than when commissioning *gas compression systems*. This is obviously due to the extremely sensitive and costly equipment involved.

Traditionally piping cleanliness is part of the Construction organization's responsibility. However repeat experience tells us this is an area where the value loss = schedule delay, is very high and hence needs to be taken extremely seriously by commissioning management.

When Construction has finished their piping assembly job, the pipes tend to be full of "shit" resulting from welding, sand blasting and the like. Very often you will not find piping completion records other than the hydro-testing records, and these do not prove the systems are clean and free of debris. Sometimes you will find Construction performing what is defined as "drop-flush", which basically consist of dropping of the pressure after a hydro- test, via a low point drain, and thereby assuming the system to be clean!

The only thing you, as the Commissioning Manager should think about here is: *Never expect to receive a clean system, and make sure you boroscope all critical systems before you accept the Hand-Over from Construction!*

Alternatively make sure Construction boroscope the systems before Hand-Over and that you witness and verify the results!

The illustration below shows the empirical value of the Piping Cleanliness schedule impact potential.

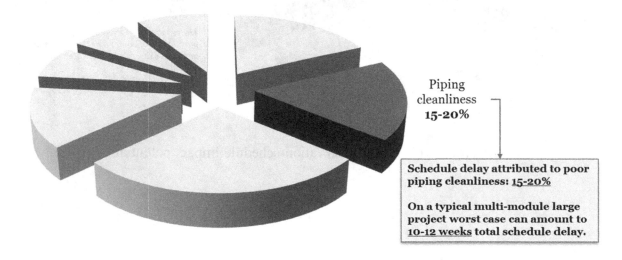

Illustration 70. Poor Piping Cleanliness- schedule impact potential

N² Test-Run of Gas Compressor Trains Onshore

As explained in the "Preparation" chapter, under the same heading as above, the schedule impact of not doing a test run of the gas compressors can be significant.

The general experience is that 10-12 weeks in offshore start-up time of the gas compression system is saved by performing the run tests during the onshore phase, at the module yard, or at the integration site (depending on system configuration and lay-out).

Normally, this also has a significant effect on oil production during the initial offshore phase because of the flaring restriction as production will have to be cut back when the associated gas is being flared rather than injected. The cost impact in terms of additional direct costs is related to having a significant number of vendor personnel and commissioning personnel on rotation for extended periods, as well as the additional logistic costs for material and personnel.

Experience figures indicate that the cost of offshore hours is slightly more than 3 times the cost of onshore hours.

The graphs below illustrate these relationships.

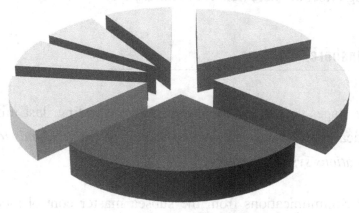

Schedule delay attributed to lack of full onshore test-run of gas compressors: <u>20-30%</u>

On a typical multi-module large project worst case can amount to <u>10-12 weeks</u> total schedule delay.

Nitrogen (N2) testing of compressor trains **20-30%**

Illustration 71. Lack of N2 Test-run of Gas Compression trains- schedule impact potential

The graph below shows how the offshore scope will suffer (grow) as a consequence of not performing N² test-runs of compressors at the onshore site. The graph illustrates the effect if *only alignment work* is performed onshore.

Onshore

Offshore

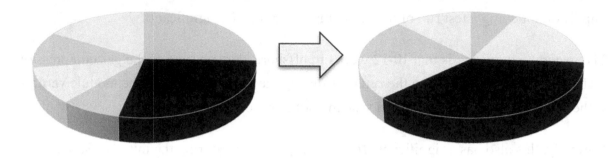

Alignment work
only

– Costly offshore
hours
– Costly logistics
– POB
restrictions =
extended
duration

– Re-alignment work
– Commissioning on
live gas (HC)
– All initial
troubleshooting
– Calibrate and set all
controls

Illustration 72. Minimizing gas compression work onshore
and resulting effect offshore (relative relationships)

Sub-Sea Simulation Testing Onshore

By detecting issues at an early stage, you will avoid costly offshore testing, last minute troubleshooting, offshore modifications and delayed start-up. *It pays great dividends to set up and test all subsea communications systems onshore.*

This testing should include all communications from the subsea master control module (normally in the Central Control Room topsides) to the sub-sea control interface cabinets and from there to a simulator acting as the sub-sea control pod with feedback facilities to topsides. This will give you a full test of the complete communication link for your subsea controls and all interfaces between the various systems.

A typical large sub-sea development project has 20 + wells, umbilicals and flowlines stretching 10 – 20 plus kilometers, has integral control systems controlling a specter of wells via subsea distribution using umbilical jumpers, etc. The value of testing all these interfaces and general communications onshore is tremendous.

A typical test on a very large and complex subsea development project will take 6-8 weeks of solid testing.

The lack of such testing onshore will obviously shift the testing to offshore, with POB limitations, first time testing, troubleshooting and modifications will easily bring the offshore duration up 8-10 weeks.

Not a very good prospect when the owners scream for hydrocarbons!

So, make sure you perform these tests onshore!

The illustration below shows the empirical value of the Onshore Subsea Simulation Testing schedule impact potential.

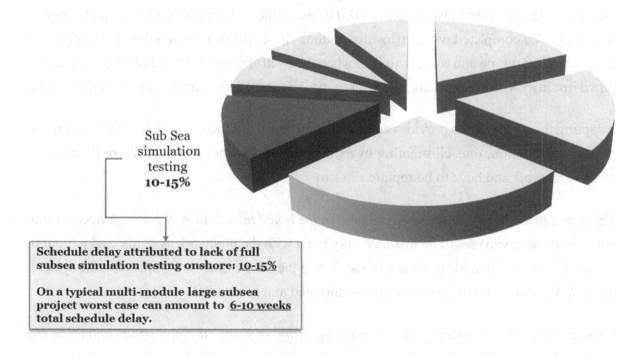

Sub Sea simulation testing **10-15%**

Schedule delay attributed to lack of full subsea simulation testing onshore: 10-15%

On a typical multi-module large subsea project worst case can amount to 6-10 weeks total schedule delay.

Illustration 73. Lack of Onshore Subsea Simulation Testing- schedule impact potential

Timing of the Installation of Main Control Valve and PSV's

In all projects there is always a considerable amount of time and monies allocated to 'control valves'. Some of these are likely to be long delivery items.

Why do we, after all the effort, install these costly valves at the early part of construction and allow them to sit in the pipework "for years" and in most cases, forget to preserve them? It is at the commissioning stage that problems are encountered, such as damaged seats due to ingress of dirt/grit, cleaning operations, damaged or scored balls due to turning and even damage during preservation. This amounts to schedule delays on the project, due to lack of foresight on *your* part.

Suggestion time: *When these expensive valves arrive on site, keep them in the stores under ideal conditions until you need them and install "bobbin" pieces in the pipework!*

These can be made with the same face-to-face dimension of the valve so as to eliminate any problems when the correct valves are fitted. The use of these "bobbins" will allow all the piping activities to be completed without any disruption. There will be time required to complete all the instrument tubing and cable activities when the control valve is fitted, however, this can be timed just prior to the N^2/He leak testing activity and subsequent commissioning of the system.

Adopting this method also provides enough time to bench test the valve under ideal conditions, prior to installation, thus eliminating overruns in the field when valves leak, or do not give positive shut off and have to be repaired in situ.

This same principle should also be adopted in the timed installation of PSV's. Under normal conditions these valves will be installed very early with the pipework systems, and left out in the field for a considerable amount of time. When the time comes to commission the system, these PSV's now need to be removed, re-calibrated and reinstalled.

Instead*: Install the 'dummy' piece or made up fitting of screwed connections and leave the PSV's in the stores. Bench test the units prior to commissioning and give the operations team a longer usage time with the fully tested and certified PSV.* Doing this will take away the need to replace or rework valves due to corrosion or damage.

The following chart shows the benefits of not installing Control Valves early as a time comparison sheet.

ID	ℹ	Task name	Dur.	Week -1	Week 1	Week 2
1		**"Normal "Conditions**	**11 days**			
2		Control valve installed early with Pipework	1 day			
3		Subjected to Pipe Flushing Open/Closing	1 day			
4		Commissioning Valve found damaged	1 day			
5		Remove Valve from pipework	1 day			
6		Change seals and or ball	2 days			
7		Subject to spares available or delivery	1 day			
8		Re-test valve	1 day			
9		Reinstall Valve, tubing and cables	2 days			
10		Re-Leak test	1 day			
11		Re-start Commissioning	1 day			
12						
13		**Suggested Method**	**7 days**			
14		Bobbin piece installed early with Pipework	1 day			
15		Pipe Flushing ongoing	1 day			
16		Bench Test Valve prior to Installation	3 days			
17		Install Control Valve, Tubing & Cables	3 days			Potential Saving: 6 days per activity
18		Start Commissioning	1 day			

Illustration 74. Control valve comparison sheet

The illustration below shows the empirical value of the poor Timing of installation of Control Valves and Pressure Relief valves- schedule impact potential.

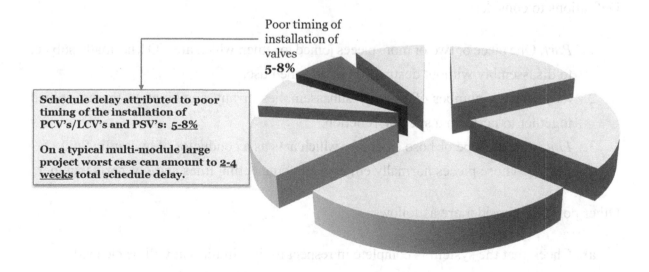

Poor timing of installation of valves
5-8%

Schedule delay attributed to poor timing of the installation of PCV's/LCV's and PSV's: 5-8%

On a typical multi-module large project worst case can amount to 2-4 weeks total schedule delay.

Illustration 75. Poor timing of the installation of Control Valves
and Pressure relief Valves- schedule impact potential

Oil Flushing of Hydraulic Systems/ Lube Oil Systems

Whether this activity is covered by Construction or Commissioning, under normal conditions it can take up to three months to have a typical system cleaned as per the NAS specification, because of all or some of the points given below. Due to the critical timing of this operation it is for practical purposes advisable *to parallel as many systems as possible* when performing these activities.

Within the specification there are two methods of measuring the contamination limits;

Practice 785 control filter gravimetric method and Practice 598 particle count method, both of which will maintain the requirements needed.

Make the decision early, check the extent of the system, materials, labor requirements, specialized equipment needed and if necessary bring in a Specialist Vendor. You must ensure that within your schedule you have prepared for this scope of work. On numerous occasions this has not been planned correctly and delays and overruns are the resultant outcome.

Over the various projects we have found it beneficial to adopt a specialist contractor to carry out this scope of the work. They will provide the pumps, hoses, specialized analysis measuring equipment and recommended cleaning fluids. It is also advisable to make the vendor responsible for the environmental conditions and disposal.

Definitions to consider:

1. *Part*: One piece or two or more pieces joined together, which are NOT normally subject to disassembly without destruction of designed use.
2. *Assembly*: A number of parts or subassemblies or any combination thereof joined together to perform a specific function.
3. *Line*: A tube, pipe or hose assembly which acts as a conductor of hydraulic fluid.
4. *Fitting*: Those pieces normally employed in connecting lines and / or parts together.

Other points to consider are as follows:

a) Check that the system is complete in respect to the circuit that will be cleaned.
b) Check that the system piping does not contain any 'dead legs'
c) Check that all flanged joints have the correct gasket fitted and all torque figures are right.

d) Check that all manual valves are included and of the correct type.

e) Check that all NDT reports are OK.

f) Check that the hydraulic calculations are correct with regards to flow and return line sizes.

g) The fluid sample size used to check the cleanliness should be proportional to the total volume of fluid contained in the system being checked.

It is imperative that once the system is cleaned to the standard required, the Commissioning department becomes the system custodian until handed over to Operations.

The illustration below shows the empirical value of poor oil Flushing- schedule impact potential.

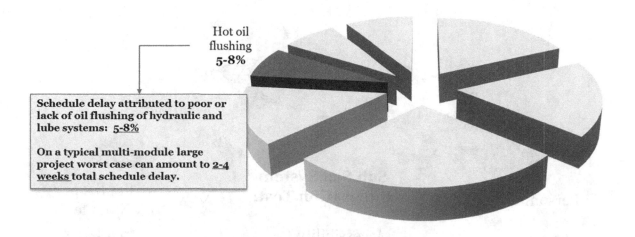

Hot oil
flushing
5-8%

Schedule delay attributed to poor or lack of oil flushing of hydraulic and lube systems: 5-8%

On a typical multi-module large project worst case can amount to 2-4 weeks total schedule delay.

Illustration 76. Poor oil flushing- schedule impact potential

Sub Sea System Integration Testing

Onshore testing of expensive subsea equipment prior to installation on the seabed is an enormous advantage now recognized by many Operators and has become the standard way of "doing things".

In harsh environments where repair work is dependent on weather, mobilization and stand-by time cost for "repair vessels" can be significant and production downtime costs can reach astronomical proportions. Definitely not what the owners are looking for.

A simple cost/benefit analysis will convince you that you need to plan for this test to take place.

The objectives of performing a System Integration Test (SIT) of sub-sea equipment prior to installation offshore are:

- Verify the operational procedures and manuals.
- Verify the physical interface between the subsystems.
- Training of personnel for the equipment and operations.
- Document the equipment and operations with photo and video records.
- Verify the ROV accessibility and operations.
- Ensure that all unique features are identified and tested.
- Increase sub-sea performance, optimize offshore scope and reduce cost.
- Verification and operation of various tools and auxiliary equipment.

The illustration below shows the various interfaces involved in a Subsea System Integration test.

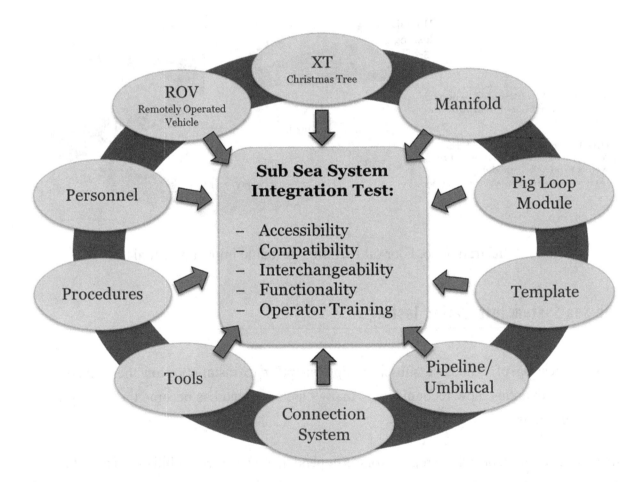

Illustration 77. Subsea Integration Testing interfaces

The illustration below shows the empirical value of Lack of/poor Subsea Integration Testing-schedule impact potential.

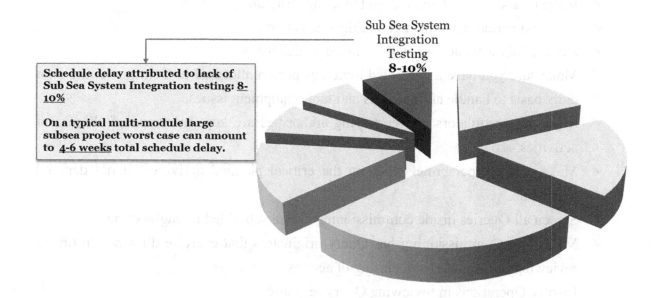

Schedule delay attributed to lack of
Sub Sea System Integration testing: <u>8-10%</u>

On a typical multi-module large subsea project worst case can amount to <u>4-6 weeks</u> total schedule delay.

Sub Sea System
Integration
Testing
8-10%

Illustration 78. Lack of/poor Subsea Integration Testing- schedule impact potential

SUMMARY-Key Success Factors in the Execution Phase

- ✓ Instigate a structured and focused meeting structure.
- ✓ Focus on variations to plan and mitigation actions.
- ✓ Always follow up actions with actionee on deadlines.
- ✓ Make sure you have a dedicated materials person allocated to Commissioning on a daily basis to handle all materials and tools/equipment issues.
- ✓ Make sure regulators and certifying authorities are kept informed of all current activities.
- ✓ Make sure all personnel work on the critical planned activities, if not demand explanations
- ✓ Screen all Queries inside commissioning before submitted to engineering
- ✓ Make sure Commissioning has Query originators that exercise diligence in timely reviewing of responses and closing of actions
- ✓ Involve Operations in reviewing Query responses.
- ✓ Make sure that commissioning exercise due diligence in timely manpower (labor) forecasting.
- ✓ Develop an authorization matrix that specifies spending levels and all relevant signatory approvals.
- ✓ Put a process in place to regularly monitor and improve on the schedule.
- ✓ Put a preservation program and an engineer in place early, make him/her accountable and dedicate resources to preservation.
- ✓ Make sure you boroscope all critical lines for cleanliness.
- ✓ Make sure the onshore compressor testing is timed to suit the required utilities.
- ✓ Make sure the use of the load banks is timed to suit the related activities.
- ✓ Make sure that testing of subsea systems are witnessed by Operations, and that all equipment to be used offshore is included in the tests
- ✓ Make sure the regulators and Certifying authorities are in attendance on all critical activities.
- ✓ Don't install control valves or pressure relief valves before the systems have been cleaned.
- ✓ Make sure the hot oil flushing activities are carried out by a competent contractor and follow up on resulting actions.

4.0. DOCUMENTATION- HANDOVER AND TAKEOVER

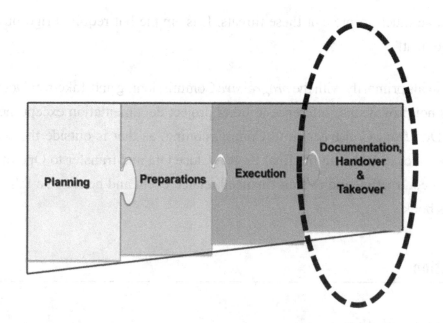

- Documentation, Handover and Take Over
- Lessons learned
- Summary: Key Success Factors in the Documentation, Handover and Take Over phase

Documentation, Handover and Takeover

Keep your books in order!

Lack of keeping Commissioning and Take Over documentation in order is a constant threat to the schedule, as this *ultimate Key Performance Indicator* (KPI) demonstrates how well you are performing relative to Take- Overs by the Operations Group.

To "scramble" all documentation after the fact is a guaranteed recipe for disaster. It will make your audit trail very dubious, and it will hinder a smooth and streamlined Take Over process jeopardizing the project schedule.

It does not take much to prevent these threats. It is simple but requires rigorous follow up from management!

This chapter deals primarily with the *progressive* Commissioning and Takeover Documentation only. It does not provide any reference to other project documentation except the important Hand Over Doc from Construction to Commissioning, as that is outside the scope of this book. Neither does it deal with the final Project Close Out and transfer to Operations as this is primarily a contractual and overall financial related event and hence also falls outside the scope of this book.

Documentation

KISS – Keep It Simple Stupid.

Documenting Commissioning activities is your QA and audit trail.

Basically, all Commissioning documentation becomes part of what you hand over to Operations at the end of the day.

The commissioning dossiers that you develop and maintain will be "converted" to a Take Over Dossier for presentation to the Operations Group when your job is done.

Time and time again, we see the failure to streamline the development and maintenance of the Commissioning Dossiers. This always leads to "last minute scrambling" to update the dossiers prior to presentation to Operations. "Last minute scrambling" is often lasting for week(s) not minutes, hence adversely affecting the schedule.

This is one of the most common schedule delay elements in the later phases of a project.

Focus should be directed at *early elimination* of this delay potential.

Commissioning engineers are normally very good at commissioning, and normally not so good at being structured when it comes to documentation. Experience has told us that it pays to employ a couple of technical clerks to help out here. The clerks can set up all the necessary Dossiers (hard copies or soft copies), make sure that the commissioning engineer (or Lead) maintain them as the work progresses, and assist in readying them for Take Over by the Operations Group. *KISS - Keep it simple stupid!*

The key to success here is simple: Set up the dossiers at the outset of commissioning and make sure they are maintained throughout! With a little dedicated assistance it should be easy!

You, as the Commissioning Manager, should demand a structured set-up from the start and make sure resources are made available to maintain the dossiers as you go. In that simple way you have eliminated a significant schedule threat.

And one more important point:

Make sure you "audit" the development of the dossiers. Make Take Over documentation status a standard agenda item in your weekly meetings. If you lose focus on it, your organization will also lose focus!

Hand Over/ Take Over

The illustration below shows the two main stages of documentation Hand Over on a project: Hand Over from Construction to Commissioning and Take Over by Operations from Commissioning.

In addition it shows the internal QA process within Construction indicating completion of disciplines within a Commissioning Package (part system) prior to issuing the Hand Over certificate.

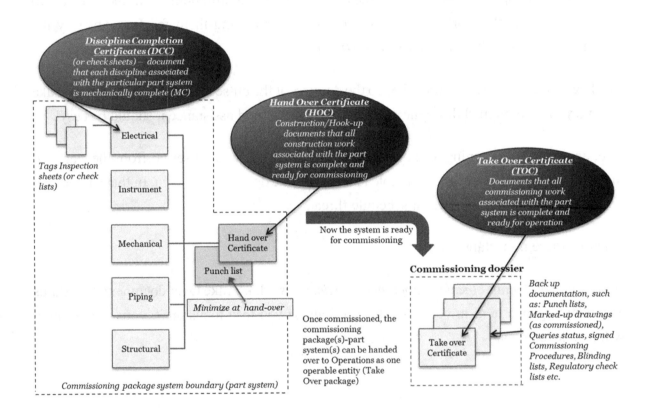

Illustration 79. Hand Over and Take Over documentation stages

Commissioning to Take Over Dossier Evolution

The illustration below shows the typical Commissioning to Take Over dossier evolution on a project.

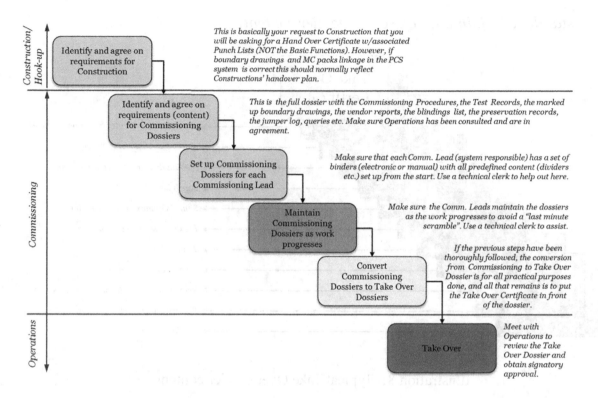

Illustration 80. Commissioning –to -Take Over dossier evolution

Take Over Dossiers

As explained on previous pages, the Take Over Dossier is a transitioning of the Commissioning Dossiers.

Based on an agreed Take Over procedure with the Operations Group, you build up the content of the Take Over Dossier.

There are different ways of setting up the Take Over Dossier, and depending on Operation's requirements, they can vary from project to project.

However, there are some "standard" elements that you should make sure are covered.

The illustration below shows a "standard" Take Over Dossier content

Take Over Dossiers

A "standard" minimum Take Over Dossier content:

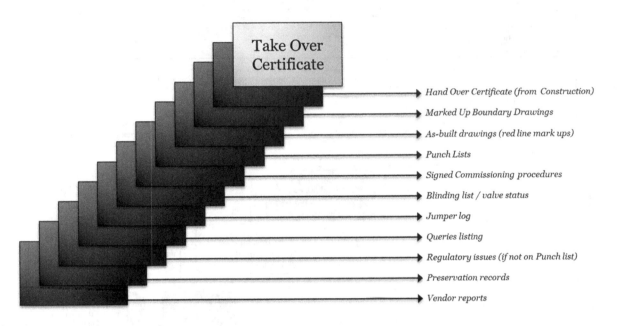

Take Over Certificate

→ *Hand Over Certificate (from Construction)*
→ *Marked Up Boundary Drawings*
→ *As-built drawings (red line mark ups)*
→ *Punch Lists*
→ *Signed Commissioning procedures*
→ *Blinding list / valve status*
→ *Jumper log*
→ *Queries listing*
→ *Regulatory issues (if not on Punch list)*
→ *Preservation records*
→ *Vendor reports*

Illustration 81. Typical Take Over dossier content

Take Over Certificate

The Take Over Certificate (TOC) signifies the Take Over from Commissioning by Operations and is signed by both parties, normally the Offshore Installation manager and the Commissioning Manager. The TOC lists all the accompanying documents that should be handed over together with the certificate itself, and as such the TOC becomes the "cover letter" for all other Take Over documentation.

Hand Over Certificate

This is the Hand Over Certificate that was handed over from Construction to Commissioning that signifies that all Mechanical Completion packages (made up of relevant Discipline

Completion Certificates) that makes up a Commissioning package is completed and accepted by Commissioning.

Marked Up Boundary Drawings

The full system marked up drawing must be included. These might be red lined if any changes have occurred during commissioning, and these changes need to be transferred to the as-built drawings.

As built drawings (red line mark ups)

These are the drawing that the actual commissioning followed including all monitored query changes relative to the Take Over in question. Normally these will be kept in the central control room (CCR) to ensure operation is in accordance with the current design. It is common practice to undergo a step by step red line-to- engineering update of drawings, and hence it is important to keep the red line mark ups in one single location (CCR) until a batch is ready for engineering update and issued as a new formal revision.

Punch lists

There are typically 3 categories or priorities of punch lists. These are "A", "B" and "C".

Upon Take Over by Operations these have the following definitions:

"A": System cannot operate with theses active. These must therefore be cleared before Take Over by Operations. Hence for all practical purposes there cannot be any "A"- items upon Take Over.

"B": Minor items that would not by definition effect the operation of the system or equipment, but would normally require a Permit to Work to be cleared, and hence could possibly disturb operation. These "B" items are typically subject to negotiations upon Take Over.

It is however interesting to observe that some Top Quartile (World Class) players do not accept *any* "B" (or of course not any "A") at all upon Take Over.

"C". These generally affect only visible appearance and are normally agreed upon Take Over to be cleared by the Operator.

Upon Final Project Handover, the financial close out of the project (not covered herein) all remaining punch list items are normally accompanied by a monetary value in the form of a lump sum budget transfer from Project to Operations. Then it is up to Operations when and how to complete this remaining scope of work.

Signed Commissioning Procedures

In practice the commissioning process comprises the integrated application of a set of techniques and procedures to check inspect and test every operational aspect of the project.

The main objective of commissioning is to affect the safe and orderly handover of each system from the construction to the end owner. In essence it is the guaranteeing of the operability in terms of performance, reliability and safety, as well as information traceability of each step in the procedures.

This is probably the most important part of the Take Over documentation as each single step of commissioning is identified and each section is signed off by the responsible commissioning engineer. All running logs are contained within these procedures along with all temperatures, pressures and flow rates recorded against all design settings. If any changes have been done to meet these design objectives they are recorded in the Query listing (Query Log).

Blinding List/Valve List

This list is held in the CCR and is maintained on a 24 hour basis. The valve status is normally registered as "closed" or "open" as the list only applies to positive isolation valves and not control valves. In cases where isolations are required at control valves, "blinds" are put in and registered.

The following blinding check list is a guideline:

- Will the blind effectively accomplish its purpose in the location selected?
- Is the blind correct material and thickness?
- Is the blind located at the flange closest to the equipment or vessel?

- Is the correct gasket for the service installed on the correct side of the flange?
- Is the selected location accessible for personnel?
- Can the blind be removed safely (purging requirements, draining etc.)?
- Has equipment lockout procedure been executed?
- Will personnel require any additional safety or protective equipment to perform operation?

Jumper log

In order to assist in the commissioning of systems, certain instrument signals sometimes need to be suppressed and hard wire jumpers are installed to achieve this. In some of the advanced control systems "soft" signals can be blocked, however, a full record must be kept to ensure control.

Query Listing

This is the Commissioning's dataset for recording all the changes to the original scope and engineered solutions to meet the requirements. Each query has a unique identifier with an originator and date when the query was implemented as well as affected systems.

All information related to the specific queries (normally identified in the Commissioning Query Register) must be documented upon Take Over.

Regulatory issues and Authority Certificates

Any regulatory issues should be recorded on the Punch List. However, some regulators, depending on country and region, require to issue own certificates recording their own activities during commissioning. Hence these must follow the Take Over documentation.

Preservation Records

During the life of a project there is equipment installed many months before it comes into use, and if preservation is not periodically executed then additional work may have to be implemented to clear the problem or in worst case replace the item (equipment). The preservation records must be maintained and have documentation going back to the company that built it, construction department that installed it and commissioning that tested it.

All preservation records for every piece of equipment will not be included in the Take Over documentation, however a reference to the traceable records must be included.

Vendor Reports

Vendor reports are unique to each vendor being used on the project. However company must decide at an early point what documentation is required. The records should start with any outstanding work or punch list items from FAT and through the whole project phase from construction to commissioning. All specific vendor reports must be logged and a list of these and where these are documented must be presented upon Take Over by Operations.

Lessons Learned

Upon completion, all projects do lessons-learned sessions in one form or another. The most prevalent scheme is to ask some of the key personnel to write lengthy "lessons learned" report that will be shelved the very minute they are written.

There are two issues with such an approach that makes it a waste of time.

First, at the tail end of the project, the key personnel have already left to go to other projects somewhere else.

Second, when you start up a new project, nobody has time to sit down and read lengthy reports from another project. No matter how good the report is, and even if someone does read it, it is far from an ideal way of transferring lessons learned.

Of course, there is no better lessons learned concept than to transfer all Project and Operations personnel from one project to the next, but as we all know, in practice, this is impossible.

How about the *KISS approach?*

During the project, you performed several risk sessions (risk analysis) that is if you adhered to the advice given in this book. These risk analysis reports now already exist in a very simple and legible format, that is again, if you took our advice.

All these risk reports tell you what could have gone wrong and what you did to mitigate the issues. Since the issues (risks) are already identified and the mitigation actions too, you've got yourself the best and most useful lessons learned report you can ever hope to get!

So, take these already existing reports, check the issues for relevance in work-sessions with your key personnel on your next project and you should be well underway to avoid repeating the same mistakes on your new project!

SUMMARY- Key Success Factors in the Documentation / Hand-over & Take Over phase

✓ Agree on the content of the Take Over packages with Operations early.

✓ Develop the Commissioning Dossiers (Take Over packages) early.

✓ Complement the Commissioning Dossiers as the work progresses.

✓ Hire a technical clerks to assist with the Commissioning Dossiers.

✓ Follow up on the Commissioning Dossiers development in the regular meetings.

✓ Involve regulators and certifying authorities to ensure compliance and signatory acceptance of activities.

✓ Use the risk analysis sessions as basis for the final lessons learned sessions.

Final comments on project overruns

Completion issues

We firmly believe, based on our experience and data, that between 80 and 90 % of the risks that materialize during the completion and commissioning phase can be prevented, and hence the resultant overruns can be prevented. The reason being as previously explained, that the majority of these risk are *generic* and from a management perspective, should have been structurally dealt with in order to minimize these.

Our experience tells us that these risks could have been removed or minimized by:

- Thorough upfront planning and preparations
- Early (FEED phase) commissioning and operations involvement. (Reduce volume of design changes)
- Put the "A-team" on the job from day 1
- Continuity among key players from phase to phase
- Use experience contingency factors when estimating
- Developing the boundary drawings early (as early as possible and based on well advanced design documentation) and define the MC packages based on these
- Early integration of construction and commissioning schedule
- Establishing the "ultimate KPIs- the Take Overs as milestones in the integrated project schedule
- Performing facilitated and repetitive practical risk sessions during project execution
- Detail follow up of critical contractors deliveries
- Organize the project completion/commissioning team in a process oriented fashion

As you can see most of these issues are purely *management related* and not technical.

This is very much in line with research on the subject of project overruns.

"Quarterly Brazil tracker" from Credit Suisse, Jan 2014- via Thomson One, and similar investigations clearly state that:

"Non-technical issues are responsible for the majority of overruns in the oil and gas industry. 65% of project failures were due to softer aspects such as people, organization and governance. A further 21% were caused by management processes and contracting and procurement strategies, with the remaining 14% of the failures due to external factors such as government intervention and environmental-related mandates"

Global project issues

Obviously, there are not only completion and commissioning issues, but also more global project issues that contribute significantly to project overruns, and we will touch on a few of the key issues below.

One of the most predominant issues is ***underdeveloped FEED*** when kicking off the project.

A thorough upfront initial design (FEED) is a prerequisite for successful project execution. Many projects seem to be governed on too ambitious plans from the outset of the project. Time allocated to FEED is too short and consequently the design basis when sanctioning the project is poorly developed. This in turn results in construction and procurement kicked off on a very poor basis, which again leads to a significant change portfolio during execution.

Directly linked to an underdeveloped FEED at project start up is also the issue of *poor decision making processes*, and/or *lack of compliance (discipline) with internal stage gate processes*, which very often leads to passing decisions gates without the proper design maturity in place, hence incurring time consuming design changes with consequential construction and commissioning growth.

Another highly contributing issue is ***contracting strategy and follow up.***

It is very important that the project has a contracting strategy that contributes to securing quality and progress. The Operators' follow up and pre-qualification of contractors/suppliers must be clearly visible in the operators' contracting strategy. Surprisingly often, this is not the case.

Close follow up of all contracts large and small is not possible. The Operator should develop a prioritizing matrix based on *project execution risk* in order to land on the most important follow up candidates, and key project personnel should be allocated to this follow up. Very often, we see "junior" engineers having this responsibility, which for the most part is a total waste of time, and does not move project risk down the scale one little bit.

Furthermore, the contractors and suppliers that fall in the lesser prioritized categories should be subject to proper prequalification routines. This will reduce the risk of change of contractors and suppliers during the course of the project, that the quality of deliveries is under par and that critical technology elements are not delivered in line with expectations.

Interface management when it comes to contractors is for obvious reasons always an issue. In addition, it always seems to be an underestimated risk. No matter how it is viewed, contracts are per global project definitions NOT stand-alone contracts even if they are from a procurement/contracting strategy point of view. Contractor's physical deliveries, i.e. equipment, will eventually come together as pieces that make up a total project design.

It is therefore well-invested time to *build effective follow up teams across contractual barriers,* a concept that seems to finally gaining momentum in some operating organizations.

Yet another popular "debating issue" is the subject of **the projects geographical placement**.

There are many *opinions* on this issue, especially the link between FPSOs from Asian yards and overruns. To our knowledge there exist no *objective* dataset that clearly shows this correlation. (Maybe because most FPSOs are built in Asia and thereby there is no real basis for comparison!). However, everyone that has had dealings with the issue, seem to agree that the FPSOs out of Asian yards have an inordinate amount of associated change orders, and most opinions seem to agree on the following reason: These yards are phenomenally experienced *hull constructors*, but significantly less professional when it comes to outfitting. Hence, the large amount of engineering changes. Although this is not accurately and precisely documented, all experience tells us that the issue can only be dealt with by making sure the design is properly advanced at contract placement and that sufficient resources are allocate to detail contract follow up at the yards.

With an ever-increasing project complexity, **Management skills** is also an issue of which interface management is a major one.

Ineffective project management is a major cause of delays. Very often, the project team fails to fully understand the critical activities and the full effect of change on the schedule and work packages. We often observe that project plans omit the required schedule management elements of schedule development, acceptance, progress measurement and reporting, and their relationships with and interdependence with other project disciplines, all leading to ineffective project management.

It is a challenge to work with multiple contractors, each with separate but often interlinked work scope, making real time data challenging to recover. This results in difficulties in measuring performance and impact of change. To overcome this issue project should set up interlinked work breakdown structures with real time data input as a pre-emptive measure and not as a response to poor project performance! There are Best Practices out there on this issue- use it!

Risk management is a subset of project management.

One significant issue is that of *continuous risk management*. Projects are normally good at running the initial risk models, especially on the big-ticket items. It is however not always the big-ticket items that make up the biggest risk on projects, it is all the other "minor" issues that pop up during the course of the project which quite often are not reflected in the project estimate.

Consequently, project management should run risk awareness sessions during the engineering phase with focus on completion risks. These should be repeated at the startup of each new project phase, and cost consequences and remedies should be identified. In addition practical risk sessions (PRS) should be run across disciplines and functions on all technical risks based on generic risk registers!

These risk sessions should be *visible milestones in the overall integrated project schedule*, which gives a tremendous compliance driver for the management team as now they also have to report progress on how they are doing against the completion of these risk sessions!

There are obviously many global issues that need attention during project planning and execution, but the issues above are the ones that we have experienced as the major items with the biggest impact on project overruns.

As you can see, all the points mentioned above fall into the 65% and 21% "soft issues" and "management issues"- categories mentioned above.

It speaks volumes of where you need to concentrate your efforts!